The
WORST-CASE SCENARIO
Survival Handbook:
TRAVEL

The
WORST-CASE SCENARIO
Survival Handbook:
TRAVEL

By Joshua Piven and David Borgenicht
Illustrations by Brenda Brown

CHRONICLE BOOKS

SAN FRANCISCO

The authors wish to thank all of the experts, whose invaluable knowledge and experience have made this book possible, and may have even saved a life or two. Special thanks and good karma to all those who worked on the book: Mindy Brown, Erin Slonaker, Jason Rekulak, Susan Van Horn, Frances J. Soo Ping Chow, Jason Mitchell, Steve Mockus, and of course, Jay Schaefer.

Library of Congress Cataloging in Publication Data available.

ISBN: 0-8118-3131-0

Printed in the United States of America

Typeset in Adobe Caslon, Bundesbahn Pi, and Zapf Dingbats

Designed by Frances J. Soo Ping Chow

a book soup publishing book
www.booksouppublishing.com
Visit www.worstcasescenarios.com

Distributed in Canada by Raincoast Books
9050 Shaughnessy Street
Vancouver, B.C. V6P 6E5

10 9 8 7 6 5 4 3 2 1

Chronicle Books LLC
85 Second Street
San Francisco, CA 94105
www.chroniclebooks.com

WARNING

When a life is imperiled or a dire situation is at hand, safe alternatives may not exist. To deal with the worst-case scenarios presented in this book, we highly recommend—insist, actually—that the best course of action is to consult a professionally trained expert. DO NOT ATTEMPT TO UNDERTAKE ANY OF THE ACTIVITIES DESCRIBED IN THIS BOOK YOURSELF. But because highly trained professionals may not always be available when the safety of individuals is at risk, we have asked experts on various subjects to describe the techniques they might employ in those emergency situations. THE PUBLISHER, AUTHORS, AND EXPERTS DISCLAIM ANY LIABILITY from any injury that may result from the use, proper or improper, of the information contained in this book. All the information in this book comes directly from experts in the situation at hand, but we do not guarantee that the information contained herein is complete, safe, or accurate, nor should it be considered a substitute for your good judgment and common sense. And finally, nothing in this book should be construed or interpreted to infringe on the rights of other persons or to violate criminal statutes: we urge you to obey all laws and respect all rights, including property rights, of others. Nonetheless, enjoy your trip.

—The Authors

CONTENTS

FOREWORD

By David Concannon, Explorers Club

During a lifetime of travel and adventure, I have learned some things the hard way—by living through many dangerous and unpleasant experiences. These experiences have taught me several very valuable lessons.

Lesson #1: The unexpected usually happens.

It was July 1989. I was standing at 15,000 feet on the side of Mt. Kilimanjaro in Tanzania, wondering if I would live.

I could still hear the voices of my friends before I left: "Kili is a cake walk. You don't need any technical climbing experience to summit. You might get a little altitude sickness, maybe a touch of edema. Don't worry, you will survive."

My thoughts were interrupted by the voice of a climbing partner, a physician, as he finished examining me. "Your lung has collapsed," he said. "You also have pulmonary and cerebral edema, and retinal hemorrhages in both eyes." Well, I thought, at least that explained the difficulty I had breathing, my new speech impediment, and the pain I felt in my eyes whenever I removed my sunglasses.

I could handle the inability to speak and the mental confusion. What really bothered me was the knowledge that I had collapsed a lung (for the second time in my life), and that my one good lung was filled with fluid. "If you get pneumonia, you will be dead by morning," the doctor said. "You better start walking."

And walk I did, for 24 miles.

Two days later, I flew in an unpressurized airplane to Kenya, followed by a flight to Germany and a horrible ride in the smoking section of a Pan Am flight to New York. After five days, I walked into a hospital in Philadelphia, where I was examined in stunned silence by a neurologist and specialist in pulmonary medicine. According to the textbooks, I shouldn't have made it. But I did. I had survived.

From that point on, I knew I could survive any worst-case scenario in my travels if I just kept my wits about me and forged ahead. Miraculously, I have always emerged from my adventures without permanent injuries, and have even been able to exit under my own power.

Lesson #2: Accept the things that are beyond your control.

Although I have not always been able to predict specifically what problems, major or minor, are going to arise, I have learned that once something does occur, I need to accept it as unavoidable. Having my pants pockets razored in Buenos Aires, being diverted through Kosovo because of "terrorist activity" in Croatia, and losing my luggage on domestic flights through Atlanta are the inevitable consequences of travel rather than extraordinary occurrences or self-inflicted mistakes.

When I was living in Kenya, I chartered airplanes to travel on weekends because flying was considered safer than driving. One time the plane I wanted to charter was booked; that weekend the plane crashed. The Kenyans reacted nonchalantly. "Hakuna ma tata," they said. "No problem. Things happen." Sometimes things happen for a reason, I thought. Sometimes they don't. But the following weekend, I took the train.

For some people, putting themselves in extreme situations and then facing the dire consequences is part of the thrill of travel. But for all types of travel, you must resign yourself to the fact that your luggage will be lost, your hotel reservations will be canceled, and the last flight out will leave without you.

The key is to then decide what you are going to do about it.

Lesson #3: Always have a contingency plan.

With a little advance preparation, you can survive the unexpected.

I once suffered from severe hypothermia thanks to an old cotton sleeping bag I carried on a backpacking trip through the White Mountains of New Hampshire. The weather forecast in the lowlands called for sunny skies and mild temperatures. Up in the mountains, however, it rained for five days straight. Everything I had was soaked, and I was never able to get warm. I eventually became delirious—and nearly unconscious.

After spending two days in another person's dry sleeping bag with two half-naked companions to restore my body temperature, I vowed I would never be caught unprepared again. I have not.

Now I research everything before I travel. I study alternative travel arrangements, accommodations, climate, travel advisories, appropriate equipment for my destination, and anything else that may be relevant. I have avoided being stranded in airports due to missed connections by knowing about later flights on competing airlines. I once traveled on eleven trains and buses to make it from Switzerland to the Hague, Netherlands, before my hostel locked its doors at midnight. (My first Swiss train was ten minutes late, and I missed every one of my original connections through Germany and the Netherlands. I still made it.) But you must be prepared. After all, a rainy day in Paris can be just as miserable as a gale in the North Atlantic if you are caught without the proper gear.

Lesson #4: No matter how bad you think things are now, they can always get worse.

I recently participated in a month-long expedition to the R.M.S. *Titanic*. The expedition provided a daily dose of Murphy's Law ("Anything that can go wrong, will"). Each day brought new and exciting challenges, sometimes several at once. Equipment failed, the weather was horrendous (we survived three gales and a hurricane), and the team was stricken with food poisoning. And all this was on top of the incredibly high level of risk we had expected to encounter.

Diving in the submersibles meant routinely facing death by implosion, drowning, fire, freezing, or asphyxiation. And to heighten the tension and discomfort, the expedition was being covered by the world's media. Nevertheless, we survived and succeeded by dealing with each challenge head-on, fixing it, and moving on to the next. We never let problems accumulate, or else we would have been overwhelmed. On our expedition or on your trip, the emphasis should not be on how bad everything is but on how to make it better, one step at a time.

Once you've learned all these lessons, you still need to know what, technically, to do. That's where this guide comes in.

People don't take trips—trips take people.
—John Steinbeck

The timorous may stay at home.
—Justice Benjamin Cardozo

INTRODUCTION

The statistics are against you: more than 50 percent of all travelers run into problems. While we hope that the worst that you'll ever encounter is a seat-back that won't recline or a dripping sink in your hotel room, there is a lot more that could go wrong.

Hijackings. Leeches. Runaway trains. Tarantulas. Tsunamis. Severed limbs. Muggings. Plane crashes. Brake failure. UFO abduction. Maybe a hotel fire while you're sleeping on the 33rd floor.

Our advice is simple: always be ready for the worst.

We don't believe that the response to the possibility of bad luck or danger is to stay home. (For one thing, as we examined in our first book, *The Worst-Case Scenario Survival Handbook*, sometimes adventure gets thrust upon you even when you are staying in and around the house.) Go out and see the world. Climb mountains, cross rivers, ride camels, sample the local cuisine, set a course for adventure—just know what to do when your travels take a turn toward disaster.

To provide you with as much help and protection as possible, we've taken an expansive view of what constitutes travel: A sandstorm might be an exotic, foreign experience if you live in New Jersey but not if you live in Saudi Arabia; if you live in Tahiti, knowing what to do if you fall onto subway tracks is a remote possibility, but if you live in Paris, New York, Tokyo, or other cities, it may well be a daily concern. A local excursion for one person might be completely foreign to another.

So for the purposes of this book, travel begins the minute you go out your front door, whether you are going across town or across the equator. These are the worst-case scenarios you could encounter, and these are the skills that could save your life.

But even though we mean well and want you to feel reassured, we are not experts in safety or survival. We are just ordinary tourists—civilians, amateurs, two regular guys (albeit regular guys with a healthy dose of paranoia and a lot of curiosity). So to deal with the threatening situations, we have again consulted experts in their fields: the U.S. Army and State Department, security specialists, pilots, railroad engineers, movie stuntpeople, counter-terrorist consultants, expedition guides, exotic creature zoologists, and demolition derby drivers, among others. (Biographies of the experts are included at the back of the book.) With their input and advice, we have constructed these illustrated, step-by-step instructions on what you need to do in dozens of dire situations.

To make this handbook useful even on less eventful days, we also asked our legions of experts to provide us with their personal, insider approach to traveling in comfort. We've compiled an appendix with select strategies for packing, flying, lodging, and traveling in general, using their collective advice and our own experience. Rounding out the appendix is a list of extreme emergency phrases (in five languages) and a selection of physical gestures to avoid, since their meaning varies widely from country to country.

If, just once, whether tomorrow or in ten years,

you are called upon to apply the information you've learned from this handbook, you could save a life—your life, or the life of someone you're with. This book could be your passport to survival. And the pages can be used as emergency toilet paper if you're really in a jam.

At the very least, it will provide good information and entertainment for the armchair survivalist.

Bon voyage.

CHAPTER 1

GETTING THERE

HOW TO CONTROL A RUNAWAY CAMEL

1 Hang on to the reins—but do not pull them back hard in an attempt to stop the camel.

A camel's head, unlike that of a wayward horse, cannot always be pulled to the side to slow it down. Camels are usually harnessed with a head halter or nose reins, and pulling on the nose reins can tear the camel's nose—or break the reins.

Hang on tight and pull the reins to one side to make the camel run in a circle. It will stop on its own.

2   If the camel has sturdy reins and a head halter, pull the reins to one side to make the camel run in a circle.

Do not fight the camel; pull the reins in the direction the camel attempts to turn its head. The camel may change direction several times during the incident— let it do so.

3   If the camel has nose reins, just hang on tight.

Use the reins for balance, and grip with your legs. If there is a saddle, hold on to the horn.

4   Hold on until the camel stops.

Whether the camel is running in circles or in a straight path, it will not run very far. The camel will sit down when it grows tired.

5   When the camel sits, jump off.

Hold on to the reins to keep it from running off.

HOW TO STOP A RUNAWAY PASSENGER TRAIN

1 Locate the emergency brake.
There is an emergency brake valve just inside each end of every passenger car. These valves are generally red and should be clearly marked.

2 Pull the handle.
This opens a valve that vents brake pipe air pressure to the atmosphere, applying the brakes for an emergency stop. There is a possibility of derailment, depending upon track curvature and grade, train weight, and the number of coaches.

IF THE BRAKE DOES NOT WORK

1 Call for help.
Locate a crew member's radio. Depress the "talk" button between the earpiece and the microphone. Do not change the channel, even if you do not hear an answer. Transmit an emergency distress call: Give any information that may help the listener understand the location of the train (for example, train number and destination). The Train Dispatcher should hear you and may clear traffic without responding. If you cannot find anyone on the radio, you will have to attempt to stop the train yourself.

2 Make your way to the front of the train.

Pull all emergency brake valves as you proceed, or instruct other passengers to apply handbrakes. These brakes are different from the red valves described earlier, and are located on each end of the passenger coach, inside the vestibule. They are applied by turning a wheel or pumping a lever. Tighten these valves as much as possible, and leave them applied.

3 Enter the locomotive.

The locomotive is usually right after the baggage car, just in front of the passenger coaches. Exercise extreme caution when stepping over and across the car couplers that connect the locomotive and baggage car.

There may be several locomotives on the train—not just one. Repeat the following steps in each locomotive. However, there is a chance that the trailing locomotive cab will be reversed, and that you will not be able to proceed any farther forward. If this is the case, retreat to the last car of the train and follow the instructions on page 26: "If the Train is Not Slowing or a Crash is Imminent."

4 Open all emergency valves located in the engine room on or near the dash (at the left side of the cab). The emergency valves will be clearly marked. Place the handles in the farthest position forward.

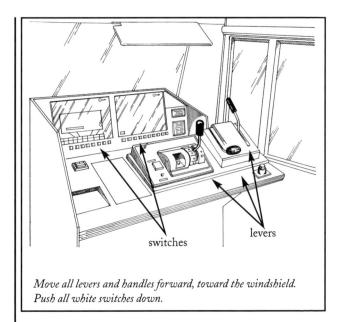

Move all levers and handles forward, toward the windshield.
Push all white switches down.

5 Move all levers and handles forward, toward the windshield.
Be certain to move the brake valves forward (they will have the word "brake" at the base of the handles). Quickly push or move down all white sliding switches on and around the control stand to shut off electricity to the engine(s).

6 If the train is still not slowing down, enter the engine room, which will be behind you to your right. A very loud engine room will indicate that the locomotive is "under load," or still operating.

7 Move rapidly through the engine room, along the engine block.

The engine block stands about four or five feet tall and looks like a large automobile engine.

8 Shut down the engine by pulling the layshaft lever.

This is a two-foot-long handle at shoulder height near the end of the engine block. It may be difficult to find, as it is not painted a different color from the engine itself. Push the handle all the way in, and the engine will run too fast and shut down. This lever is mechanical and will shut down the engine without fail.

9 Return to the cab and sound the whistle to warn others of your approach—it may take several miles to stop the train completely.

The whistle is either a handle the size of your hand that points upward, or a button located on the control panel marked "horn."

If the Train Is Not Slowing or a Crash Is Imminent

1 Proceed as calmly and quietly as possible to the rear of the train.
This is the safest place to be in the event of a crash. Instruct the other passengers to move to the back of the train with you.

2 Prepare for a crash.
Sleeping cars are usually placed on the tail end of the train and have mattresses and pillows that can be used for protection. Sit or lay against a wall that is toward the leading end of the train, so you will not fly forward in the event of a crash. The farther you are from the locomotive the better.

HOW TO STOP A CAR WITH NO BRAKES

1 Begin pumping the brake pedal and keep pumping it.

You may be able to build up enough pressure in the braking system to slow down a bit, or even stop completely. If you have anti-lock brakes, you do not normally pump them—but if your brakes have failed, this may work.

2 Do not panic—relax and steer the car smoothly.

Cars will often safely corner at speeds much higher than you realize or are used to driving. The rear of the car may slip; steer evenly, being careful not to over-correct.

3 Shift the car into the lowest gear possible and let the engine and transmission slow you down.

4 Pull the emergency brake—but not too hard.

Pulling too hard on the emergency brake will cause the rear wheels to lock, and the car to spin around. Use even, constant pressure. In most cars, the emergency brake (also known as the hand brake or parking brake) is cable operated and serves as a fail-safe brake that should still work even when the rest of the braking system has failed. The car should slow down and, in combination with the lower gear, will eventually stop.

Sideswiping guardrails or rocks may help slow you down. Do this only at slower speeds.

5 If you are running out of room, try a "bootlegger's turn."

Yank the emergency brake hard while turning the wheel a quarter turn in either direction—whichever is safer. This will make the car spin 180 degrees. If you were heading downhill, this spin will head you back uphill, allowing you to slow down.

6 If you have room, swerve the car back and forth across the road.

Making hard turns at each side of the road will decrease your speed even more.

7 If you come up behind another car, use it to help you stop.
Blow your horn, flash your lights, and try to get the driver's attention. If you hit the car, be sure to hit it square, bumper to bumper, so you do not knock the other car off the road. This is an extremely dangerous maneuver: It works best if the vehicle in front of you is larger than yours—a bus or truck is ideal—and if both vehicles are traveling at similar speeds. You do not want to crash into a much slower-moving or stopped vehicle, however.

8 Look for something to help stop you.
A flat or uphill road that intersects with the road you are on, a field, or a fence will slow you further but not stop you suddenly. Scraping the side of your car against a guardrail is another option. Avoid trees and wooden telephone poles: They do not yield as readily.

9 Do not attempt to sideswipe oncoming cars.

10 If none of the above steps has enabled you to stop and you are about to go over a cliff, try to hit something that will slow you down before you go over.
This strategy will also leave a clue to others that someone has gone over the edge. But since very few cliffs are sheer drops, you may fall just several feet and then stop.

HOW TO STOP A RUNAWAY HORSE

1 Hold on tight to the saddle with your hands and thighs.

Most injuries occur when the rider is thrown, falls, or jumps off the horse and hits the ground or some immovable object, such as a tree or fence post.

2 Grip the saddle horn or the front of the saddle with one hand and the reins with the other.

If you have lost hold of the reins, hold on to the saddle horn or the horse's mane and wait for the horse to slow or stop.

3 Sit up in the saddle as much as you can.

Fight the instinct to lean forward (it will be especially strong if you are in a wooded area with many trees and branches), since this is not the standard position for a rider when the horse is asked to stop (*whoa!*), and the horse can feel the difference. Keep a deep seat, with your feet pushed a little forward in the stirrups.

4 Alternately tug and release the reins with a medium pressure.

Never jerk or pull too hard on the reins of a horse running at full speed—you could pull the horse off-balance, and it may stumble or fall. There is a very high risk of serious injury or death if the horse falls while running at full speed (25 to 30 mph).

5 When the horse slows down to a slow lope or a trot, pull one rein to the side with steady pressure so that the horse's head moves to the side, toward your foot in the stirrup.

This maneuver will cause the horse to walk in a circle. The horse will become bored, sense that you are in control again, and slow to a near stop.

6 When the horse is at a walk, pull back with slow, steady pressure on both reins until the horse stops.

7 Dismount the horse immediately, before it has a chance to bolt again.

Hold the reins as you get down to keep the horse from moving.

Be Aware

- Long reins dangling in front of a horse may cause it to trip. Inexperienced riders should tie the ends of the reins together so that they cannot fall past the horse's neck and pose added danger.
- Horses bolt when they are frightened or extremely irritated. The key response is to remain in control of the situation without causing the horse greater anxiety. Talk to it reassuringly and rub its neck with one hand. Yelling, screaming, and kicking the horse will only make it more agitated.

HOW TO CRASH-LAND A PLANE ON WATER

These instructions apply to small passenger propeller planes (not commercial airliners).

1 Take your place at the controls.

If the plane has dual controls, the pilot will be in the left seat. Sit on the right. If the plane has only one set of controls and the pilot is unconscious, remove the pilot from the pilot's seat. Securely fasten your seat belt.

2 Put on the radio headset (if there is one) and call for help.

There will be a control button on the yoke (the plane's steering wheel) or a CB-like microphone on the instrument panel. Depress the button to talk, release it to listen. Say "Mayday! Mayday!" and give your situation, destination, and plane call numbers (which should be printed on the top of the instrument panel). If you get no response, try again on the emergency channel, 121.5. The person on the other end should be able to talk you through proper landing procedures. If you cannot reach someone to talk you through the landing process, you will have to do it alone.

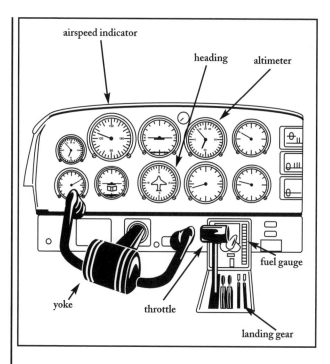

airspeed indicator

heading   altimeter

fuel gauge

yoke   throttle

landing gear

3 Get your bearings and identify the instruments.

YOKE. This is the steering wheel, and it should be in front of you. The yoke turns the plane and controls its pitch. Pull back on the column to bring the nose up, push forward to point it down. Turn it left to turn the plane left, turn it right to turn the plane right. The yoke is very sensitive—move it only an inch or two in either direction to turn the plane. While cruising, the nose of the plane should be about three inches below the horizon.

ALTIMETER. This is the most important instrument, at least initially. It is a black-faced dial in the middle of the panel with white hands and numerals, with zero at the top. The small hand indicates feet above sea level in thousand-foot increments, the large hand in hundreds.

HEADING. This is a compass. It will be the only instrument with a small image of a plane in the center. The nose of the image will point in the direction the plane is headed.

AIRSPEED. This dial is on the top of the instrument panel and will be on the left. It is usually calibrated in knots, though it may also have miles per hour. A small plane travels at about 120 knots while cruising. Anything under 70 knots in the air is dangerously close to stall speed. (A knot is $1^{1}/_{4}$ mph.)

TACHOMETER. This instrument (not visible in ill., but located near the throttle) displays the engine's power in revolutions per minute (rpm). In more sophisticated aircraft, a manifold pressure gauge may be present. This gauge supplies manifold pressure in inches of mercury, and shows you how much power an engine is producing. If present, it should be used in place of the tachometer. (One inch of mercury equals approximately 100 rpm; 10 inches corresponds to 1,000 rpm.)

Throttle. This lever controls airspeed (power) and also the nose attitude, its relation to the horizon. It sits between the seats and is always black. Pull it toward you to slow the plane and cause it to descend, push it away from you to speed up the plane and cause it to ascend.

Fuel. The fuel gauges will be on the lower portion of the instrument panel. If the pilot has followed FAA regulations, the plane should have enough fuel for the amount of flying time to your intended destination, plus at least an additional half hour of reserve. Some planes have a reserve fuel tank in addition to the primary one, but do not attempt to change tanks. Full tanks will provide $4\frac{1}{2}$ to 5 hours of flying time for a light aircraft. If the gauge indicates the tanks are half full, you will have half that time. However, be advised that fuel gauges on airplanes can be inexact and experienced pilots do not rely on them. Always assume you have a fuel emergency despite what the fuel gauge may indicate. You want to land the plane as soon as possible to avoid an uncontrolled landing.

Mixture control. This is a red knob or lever on the instrument panel, or between the pilot and co-pilot positions. The knob regulates fuel flow to the engine. Pull it out (toward you) to reduce fuel flow, push it in (away from you) to increase it.

Autopilot. The autopilot panel will be on the lower third of the instrument panel and will generally be to the immediate left or right of the yoke. There will be an on/off switch and separate switches or buttons reading "alt," "heading," and "nav."

Flaps. The flaps are the moveable parts of the wings that are used to change the speed of the plane and adjust its altitude. Due to their complexity, wing flaps can make the plane hard to control. Use the throttle to control airspeed instead.

4 If the plane is flying straight and level, engage the autopilot.
Press the "alt" (altitude) and heading buttons until the displays read "hold." This will maintain your present altitude and heading and give you an opportunity to continue to use the radio and assess your landing choices.

5 Once you have determined your landing strategy, turn the autopilot off and reduce power by moving the throttle toward you.
Slowly move the throttle enough to cause the nose to drop and the plane to descend slightly. You will need to be at approximately 2,000 feet to be able to clearly see the water below you.

6 When the altimeter reads 2,000 feet, level the nose with the horizon using the yoke.
Increase power slightly by moving the throttle away from you if pulling back on the yoke does not work.

7 Assess the water ahead of you.

It is imperative that you land in calm water and that you avoid landing the plane in the face of swells, where there is a significant risk of waves breaking over the aircraft. The plane should be heading into the wind (called a headwind), so you land on the backside of any waves.

8 Reduce power by moving the throttle toward you.

Do not use your flaps or your landing gear, which might catch on the water. Bring the plane to an altitude of 100 to 200 feet.

9 Continue to reduce power until the tachometer reads 1,500 to 1,700 rpm or 15 to 17 inches of mercury.

10 Move the nose of the plane up at least 5 to 10 degrees above the horizon by pulling the yoke toward you slightly.

You must exercise a nose-up landing to keep the propeller out of the water and prevent the plane from flipping end-over-end. The angle of the nose should be such that the horizon is almost completely obscured.

11 Just before touchdown, make sure the throttle is in its furthest position toward you.

The plane should be no more than 10 feet above the water at this point.

12 Pull the red fuel mixture control knob toward you to cut fuel to the engine when the plane is about five feet above the water.

Use the surface of the water, not the altimeter, to judge your altitude at this low level.

13 Keep the nose up by pulling back gently on the yoke. The plane should fall gently onto the water. Concentrate on making sure the rear of the plane hits the water first. If the plane has non-retractable landing gear, it will most likely flip over because the landing gear will catch on the water.

14 Open the door or window as soon as you hit the water, and quickly get out of the plane.

It may be difficult to open the door or window once you begin to sink. If you are unable to open the cabin door, kick out the windshield.

15 If the plane has life vests or a raft, inflate them outside of the plane.

The plane's emergency location transmitter (ELT) should continue broadcasting your location to rescue personnel.

HOW TO SURVIVE
AN AIRPLANE CRASH

To Decrease the Odds of a Crash

1 Take a nonstop flight, if possible.
Most accidents happen in the takeoff and landing
phases of flight; the fewer stops you make, the less
chance of an accident.

2 Watch the skies.
Many accidents involve severe weather. As takeoff
time approaches, check the weather along the route,
particularly in places where you will land. Consider
delaying your flight if the weather could be severe.

3 Wear long-sleeved shirts and long pants made of
natural fibers.
Radiant heat and flash burns can be avoided if you put
a barrier between you and the heat. Avoid easy-care
polyester or nylon: most synthetic materials that aren't
specifically treated to be fire resistant will melt at relatively low temperatures (300 to 400 degrees Fahrenheit). Synthetic fabrics will usually shrink before they
melt, and if they are in contact with skin when this
happens, they will make the burn—and its treatment—much more serious. Wear closed-toe, hard-
soled shoes; you might have to walk through twisted,
torn metal or flames. In many cases, people survive the
crash, but are killed or injured by post-impact fire and
its by-products, like smoke and toxic gases.

4 Select a seat on the aisle, somewhere in the rear half of the cabin.

The odds of surviving a crash are higher in the middle-to-rear section compared to the middle-to-front section of the cabin. An aisle seat offers the easiest escape route access, unless you are sitting right next to an emergency exit: If you can get a window seat right next to the emergency exit, this is a better choice.

5 Listen to the safety briefing and locate your nearest exits.

Most airplane accident survivors had listened to the briefing and knew how to get out of the plane. Pick an exit to use in an emergency, and an alternate in case the first one is not available.

6 Count the seats between you and the exits in case smoke fills the plane and you cannot see them.

Make sure you understand how the exit doors work and how to operate them.

7 Practice opening your seat belt a few times.

Many people mistakenly try to push the center of the buckle rather than pull up on it.

To Prepare for a Crash

1 Make sure that your seat belt is tightly fastened and that your chair back is fully upright.

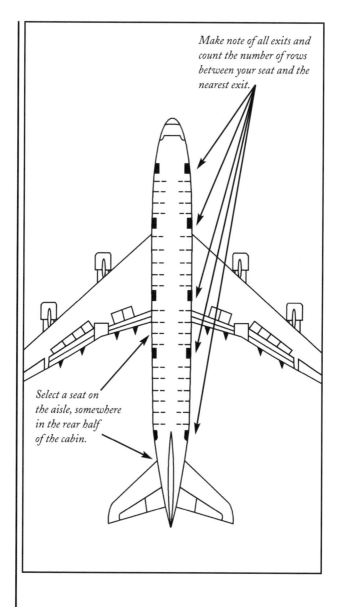

Make note of all exits and count the number of rows between your seat and the nearest exit.

Select a seat on the aisle, somewhere in the rear half of the cabin.

2 Bend forward with one arm across your knees.

3 Place your pillow in your lap and hold your head against the pillow with your free arm.

4 Push your legs forward and brace for impact by placing your feet or knees against the chair in front of you.
If you are over water, loosen your shirt (and tie) so that your movement is not restricted when you attempt to swim. Be ready for two jolts: when the plane first hits water and when the nose hits water again.

5 Stay calm and be ready to help yourself.
The vast majority of crash survivors were able to get out either under their own power or with the help of someone already on the plane. Fire and rescue personnel are unlikely to enter the airplane to pull you out.

6 Do not take anything with you.
If you have something you absolutely cannot part with, you should keep it in your pocket and not in your carry-on baggage.

7 Stay low if the plane is on fire.
Follow the exit procedures described in the safety briefing. Illuminated floor lights should indicate the exits: the lights are red where exit rows exist.

CHAPTER 2

PEOPLE SKILLS

HOW TO
SURVIVE A RIOT

1 Remain indoors if you learn about any nearby rioting or civil unrest.

Avoid the windows. Listen for reports on radio or television. If you hear gunfire, try to find out where the shooting is located. Use the telephone if it is still functioning, or ask an official or your hotel manager for information.

2 If you believe the crisis is unresolvable or seriously threatens your life, plan to leave the country quickly.

3 Determine the best route to the airport or embassy, and leave the building through any safe exit.

Make sure that the airport is operating before you travel there. If you cannot make it to your own country's embassy, plan to head for the embassy of an allied nation.

4 Wear clothing in muted tones.

Put on a long-sleeve shirt, jacket, jeans, a hat, socks, and lightweight boots. (Although you may be in a tropical or warm part of the world, it gets quite cold on planes, and you may have to sleep in an airport or connect to a flight landing in a colder region.)

5 Exit away from gunfire or mobs.

Select a way out that is not easily observed. Exits include windows, vents, or even the roof.

6 | Leave as a group.
Especially if you have to dash across an open area, such as the front of a building, a wide street, or a plaza, you are safer with company. Snipers or enemies will have multiple objects to focus on, not just one, and will not be as likely to make a move.

7 | Do not run.
Unless your life is in imminent danger, walk. Walking is harder for the eye to detect: The human eye can quickly sight someone running. Running can also generate excitement—people may chase you.

8 | If you must travel by car, be prepared for evasive maneuvers.
Drive on back streets, not main roads, and be prepared to abandon the car if the situation becomes critical. Watch out for checkpoints, roundabouts, major intersections, and military/police barracks. Do not stop for anything—remember the car can be a useful 2,000-pound weapon that even a mob cannot stop. If you cannot drive forward, drive in reverse.

A reliable driver who knows the area will be able to navigate much better than you. If no driver or taxi is available, hire a local to drive your car for you. (You may need to promise to give your car in exchange.) Abandon the car outside the embassy or airport.

If a Molotov cocktail (flammable liquid in a glass container with a lighted wick) hits your car, speed up—it may burn out as you gain speed.

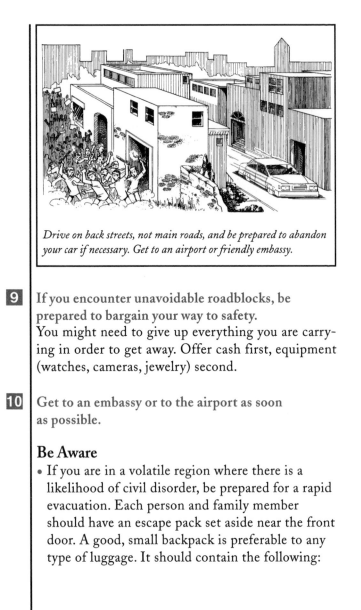

Drive on back streets, not main roads, and be prepared to abandon your car if necessary. Get to an airport or friendly embassy.

9 If you encounter unavoidable roadblocks, be prepared to bargain your way to safety.
You might need to give up everything you are carrying in order to get away. Offer cash first, equipment (watches, cameras, jewelry) second.

10 Get to an embassy or to the airport as soon as possible.

Be Aware

- If you are in a volatile region where there is a likelihood of civil disorder, be prepared for a rapid evacuation. Each person and family member should have an escape pack set aside near the front door. A good, small backpack is preferable to any type of luggage. It should contain the following:

Flashlight. Pack a mini-flashlight with extra batteries. Affix a red or blue lens if you have one; red or blue light is difficult for observers (snipers, mobs) to see at night.

Small compass and a detailed map of the city. Be sure to mark the embassy and helicopter landing zones on the map.

Knife. Include a small pocketknife for cutting.

Fire-starting tool. Carry storm-safe matches or a lighter in a waterproof bag. Pack small baggies of dryer lint, which is light and highly flammable.

Black garbage bags. Use these for emergency shelter and camouflage.

Water and food. Carry at least two quarts of water per person. Bring only high-energy or instant foods. Do not eat unless you have water.

- Conceal on your person, in a multi-pocket neck pouch, the following items:

Money. Take $25 in single U.S. dollars and all of your local currency and divide it among your pouch and pockets. This will serve as bribe money for checkpoints. Dole it out in heaps until it appears you have no more. Do not offer your papers. Carry more money in your neck pouch, but keep the bulk of your cash in your socks, crotch, or ankle pouch.

PASSPORT. Place a full photocopy of your passport in the main section of the pouch for easy access. Keep your original passport in a separate section. Show the copy to locals who demand it. Never give up the original.

OFFICIAL DOCUMENTS. Visas, phone numbers, proof of citizenship, birth certificates, and so on should be kept with your original passport.

SOFT EARPLUGS. Helicopters are very noisy, and earplugs are useful when you want to sleep in a battle zone.

HOW TO SURVIVE A HOSTAGE SITUATION

Terrorists need to exercise power and control, and they do this by turning their victims into objects, which are easier to mistreat. Follow these tips to avoid mistreatment or worse.

1 Stay calm.
Help others around you to do the same—remember that the hostage takers are extremely nervous and scared. Do not do anything to make them more so. Do not speak to them unless they speak to you.

2 If shots are fired, keep your head down and drop to the floor.
If you can, get behind something, but do not move far—your captors may think that you are attempting to make an escape or an attack.

3 Do not make any sudden or suspicious movements.
Do not attempt to hide your wallet, passport, ticket, or belongings.

4 Comply with all demands.
Hesitation on your part may get you killed instantly, or may mark you for later retribution or execution. Remain alert and do not try to escape or be a hero. If you are told to put your hands over your head, to keep your head down, or to get into another body position,

do it. It may be uncomfortable, but do not change your position on your own. Talk yourself into relaxing into the position—you may need to stay that way for some time. Prepare yourself both mentally and emotionally for a long ordeal.

5 | Never look at a terrorist directly or raise your head until you are directed to speak to him or her.
Always raise your hand and address the hostage takers respectfully. When answering questions, be respectful but not submissive. Speak in a regulated tone of voice.

6 | Never challenge a hostage taker.
They often look for potential execution victims, and if you act contrary in any way, they may select you.

7 | Carefully observe the characteristics and behavior of the terrorists.
Give them nicknames in your mind so that you can identify them. Be prepared to describe them by remembering attire, accents, facial characteristics, or height—any aspect that might later help authorities.

8 | If you are the victim of a skyjacking, know where the plane's closest emergency exits are located.
Count the rows between you and the exit. In the event of an emergency rescue, smoke may obscure visibility, and you must know the fastest path out of the aircraft. Do not attempt escape unless it is clear that a massacre is imminent.

9 If a rescue team enters, get down and stay still. Shots may be fired, and any sudden movements may draw terrorist or friendly fire.

10 Upon resolution, be prepared to identify yourself and terrorists to the rescuers. Some terrorists may try to exit with you, posing as hostages.

Be Aware

- To avoid making yourself attractive to terrorists, try not to take out your passport in public places.
- Be especially alert at airports, train stations, bus stations, in lobbies of expensive hotels, and in stores that cater to affluent tourists. While civil strife and guerrilla activity usually focus on nationals—thus tourists are relatively safe— terrorists often choose targets that will get them the most attention.

HOW TO PASS A BRIBE

1 If you are hassled by an official, be friendly, but aloof.

Do not show concern or act surly. Remain calm and good-natured. Try to determine if there is an actual problem or if the official is seeking some additional, unofficial compensation.

2 Never blatantly offer a bribe.

If you have misinterpreted the official's intentions, you may get yourself in additional trouble by overtly offering a bribe.

3 If you are accused of an infraction, ask to pay a fine on the spot.

Say that you would rather not deal with the mail or go to another location, citing your fear that the payment will get lost. Mention that you want to make sure the money gets to the proper person.

4 Try to speak to and deal with only one official.

Speak to the person who acts as though he/she is in charge. If you offer money to a junior officer while a superior is present, the superior may demand more.

5 Offer to make a "donation" to the official's organization.

Say that you would like to pay for gas, uniforms, car repairs, expenses, or other needs.

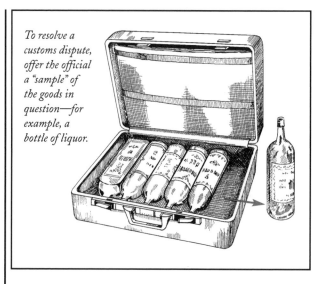

To resolve a customs dispute, offer the official a "sample" of the goods in question—for example, a bottle of liquor.

6 If you do not have cash, be prepared to offer goods instead.

Watches, cameras, and other electronics are often accepted as bribes. You might consider offering goods instead of cash even if you have the money, particularly if the "problem" concerns these goods. If, for example, a customs official tells you that you are transporting too many bottles of liquor, you might speed your trip and lighten your load by offering some of the items in dispute to the official.

Be Aware

• Carry only a small amount of money in your wallet and hide the rest. This will prevent an unscrupulous official from seeing your entire wad.

HOW TO FOIL A SCAM ARTIST

Con artists come in all shapes and sizes. In order to thwart them, you need to understand how they most commonly work. Here are a few of the most common scams, with instructions on how to avoid falling victim to them.

LUGGAGE GRAB

How the scam works

This airport scam involves two people. Scam Artist #1 gets in front of you on the line for the metal detector. You place your bags on the X-ray machine's conveyer belt. Scam Artist #2 abruptly cuts ahead of you in the line. Scam Artist #2 has lots of change and other metal objects in his pockets. You wait as he empties his pockets and goes through the metal detector several times until it stops beeping. Meanwhile, Scam Artist #1 grabs your bag as if it were his own and makes off with it. When you finally get through the metal detector, your bag is gone, and neither man is anywhere to be found.

How to foil the scam

1 Carry a bag that is distinctive and difficult to mistake for another.

2 Know what to expect.
Orderly lines may not be the norm in all countries. In some places, pushing and shoving are more accepted, which makes the scammers' job easier.

3 Never let valuables out of your sight.
Angle your body so you are able to see the far end of the X-ray machine.

4 Do not allow anyone to cut in front of you at the metal detector once you place your items on the conveyor belt.

5 Watch your luggage and be assertive with security and customs officials.

6 If you are traveling with one or more companions, do not go through the metal detector one after another.
Space yourselves several people apart, and give the majority of your valuables to the last person passing through. The first person through can watch the X-ray machine until the bag with your valuables appears.

PASSPORT AND CREDIT CARD COPY

How the scam works
When you present a traveler's check to a merchant, the merchant asks to see your passport to make sure the signatures match. She says the signatures do not match, and asks to photocopy your passport and a

credit card as proof of identification. She copies your information and uses it for unauthorized charges at a later date.

How to foil the scam

1 Always sign traveler's checks in front of the merchant.
She cannot claim the signature is forged if she watched you sign the check.

2 Never allow your credit cards or passport to be photocopied.

3 Pay cash, or leave the store immediately.

CARDBOARD CHILDREN

How the scam works
Small bands of children (usually 6 to 10 of them) confront you for change. The children swarm you, beg loudly for money or candy, while at the same time pressing pieces of cardboard against your body. The shouting distracts you, while the cardboard desensitizes you to the small hands entering your pockets or bags. The scam takes just a few seconds at most. The children suddenly disperse in different directions, taking your valuables with them. Even if you were to realize you had been robbed, you would have no way of knowing which child to follow.

How to foil the scam

1 If you are alone and are approached by a group of begging children, get to a well-populated area. Walk into the nearest store or restaurant.

2 If there is no place to hide, hold your wallet tightly in your hand so that it cannot be snatched. Even better, distribute your money in multiple pockets beforehand.

3 Make as loud a scene as you can.

Be Aware

• A money belt or waist pouch, while better than a wallet for securing valuables, can be breached by experienced thieves. If you wear a waist pouch, always make sure it faces forward and is not worn as a "fanny" pack.

• Keep your passport in a hotel safe and carry a photocopy. If you must travel with an original passport, secure it inside a pocket with a safety pin.

HOW TO FOIL
A UFO ABDUCTION

1 Do not panic.
The extraterrestrial biological entity (EBE) may sense your fear and act rashly.

2 Control your thoughts.
Do not think of anything violent or upsetting—the EBE may have the ability to read your mind. Try to avoid mental images of abduction (boarding the saucer, anal probes); such images may encourage them to take you.

3 Resist verbally.
Firmly tell the EBE to leave you alone.

4 Resist mentally.
Picture yourself enveloped in a protective shield of white light, or in a safe place. Telepathic EBEs may get the message.

5 Resist physically.
Physical resistance should be used only as a last resort. Go for the EBE's eyes (if they have any)—you will not know what its other, more sensitive areas are.

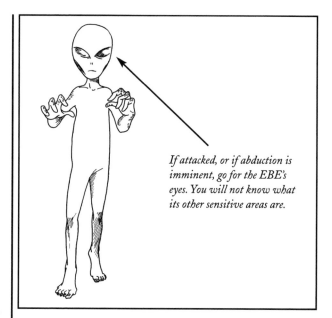

If attacked, or if abduction is imminent, go for the EBE's eyes. You will not know what its other sensitive areas are.

How to Report a UFO Sighting

1 Stay calm.
If you become upset or excited, you are likely to forget important details.

2 Accurately record the time at the start of the sighting, the time of any change of direction in the UFO's flight pattern, and the time at the end of the sighting.
If possible, use a mechanical stopwatch, since close proximity to a UFO may prevent electronic instruments from functioning correctly.

3 Sketch a schematic of the UFO's path in the ground. Mark your position in the ground at the start of the sighting, and draw a line in the direction of the object when first seen, for each direction change, and when last seen.

4 Try to identify any horizon landmarks with regard to the UFO's position.

5 If you have a video or still camera, record the sighting.
Neither video nor still images carry much weight on their own, so it is essential that the images include reference information such as a tree, a mountain, or a skyline.

6 Report the sighting as soon as possible.
Contact the UFO Reporting and Information Service (206-721-5035), the Mutual UFO Network (830-379-2166), or the National UFO Reporting Center (206-722-3000).

Be Aware
• Most sightings are in rural areas, away from bright lights, and near military installations. They occur most frequently during the summer months, around 9:00 P.M., with a secondary peak at around 3:00 A.M.

HOW TO SURVIVE
A MUGGING

1 Do not argue or fight with a mugger unless your life is clearly in danger.

If all a mugger wants is your purse, wallet, or other belongings, surrender them. Your possessions are not worth your life.

2 If you are certain that your attacker means to do you or a loved one harm, attack vital areas of your assailant's body.

Aim to disable him or her with the first blow by:

- Thrusting your fingers into and above your attacker's eyes.
- Driving your knee in an upward direction into his groin (if mugger is male).
- Grabbing and crushing the attacker's testicles as if crushing a handful of grapes (if mugger is male).
- Striking the front of his or her throat, using the area between your thumb and first finger, or the side of your hand, held straight and strong.
- Slamming the tip of your elbow into the side of the mugger's ribs.
- Stomping down on the mugger's instep.

3 Use an object as a weapon.

Many common objects can be effective weapons if they are aimed at vulnerable body parts. Pick up and use what is easily available:

- A stick can jab at an attacker's eyes or groin.
- Keys held between your fingers can slash or punch.
- A car antenna can jab or slash your attacker's face and eyes.

HOW TO
TAIL A THIEF

1 Before attempting to follow someone who
you believe has stolen from you, try to alter your
appearance.
Remove your jacket, if you were wearing one; remove
your shirt, if you are wearing a T-shirt underneath;
put on or remove a hat or sunglasses. You do not want
the thief to recognize you.

2 Never stare directly at the person you are following.
You can observe the person without being obvious.
Never make eye contact.

3 Note the thief's identifying characteristics (dress,
gait, height, and weight).
You will be able to keep track of the thief in a crowd
(or after losing sight of him or her) if you are looking
for particular details.

4 Stay well behind the person you are following.
Never tail a person by walking right behind him or
her. Follow from a distance of at least 40 feet, or from
across the street.

5 If the thief goes into a store, do not follow.
Remain outside, looking in the store window, or wait
a few doors down for the thief to come out. If the
thief does not emerge quickly, check for a back exit.

6 Once you have determined that the thief has arrived at his or her destination, call the authorities. Confronting thieves alone is risky. Use a phone or ask a storeowner to call the police. Describe your target and his or her location.

Be Aware

- Wallet thieves and pickpockets often follow a similar pattern: They pass the wallet to another person immediately following the theft in order to throw you off the trail, and that person passes it to another. If you can, follow the initial thief: The thief may no longer be carrying your wallet, but might lead you to those who are.

HOW TO LOSE SOMEONE WHO IS FOLLOWING YOU

If You Are in a Car

1 Determine if you are actually being followed.

If you suspect a tail, observe the car as you continue to drive. If the car remains behind you, make three to four turns in a row to see if it continues to follow you. Then signal a turn in one direction but turn quickly in the other direction. See if the other car turns as well.

2 Once you are certain you are being followed, get on a highway, or drive to a populous and active area.

Do not drive home, to a deserted place, or down an alley. You are more likely to shake your tail in a crowd than in a deserted area.

3 Drive at the speed limit, or a bit slower.

Soon, another car (not that of your pursuer) will attempt to pass you. Speed up slightly so the car pulls in behind you. Repeat, but don't go so slowly that an innocent car behind you is able to pass you.

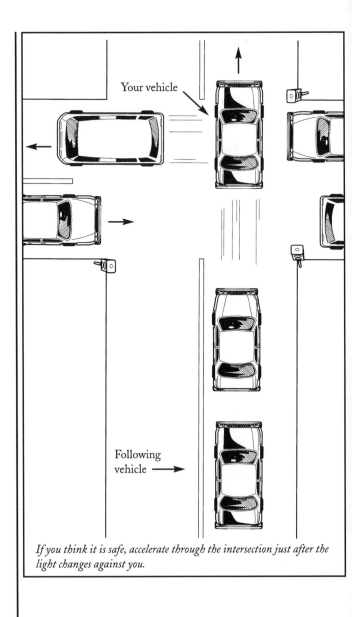

Your vehicle

Following
vehicle →

*If you think it is safe, accelerate through the intersection just after the
light changes against you.*

4 | Slow down at a busy intersection with a traffic light, then accelerate through the intersection just after the light changes.
The car following you may get stuck at the red light. If you attract the attention of the police for running a red light, your pursuer will most likely leave the scene.

5 | When you have several cars around you, speed up, get off the highway (if you are on one), and make several quick turns to further elude your pursuer.
Your pursuer should be too far back to follow closely.

6 | Once you are out of sight of your pursuer, pull into a parking lot, a garage, or a shopping center with lots of other cars.

7 | If you still have not lost your tail at this point, drive to a police station and get help.

IF YOU ARE ON FOOT

1 | Determine if you are being followed, and identify your tail.
Take a random path: Make unexpected changes in direction at intersections and retrace your steps, effectively making a U-turn. Do not, however, get yourself disoriented or lost. Note any identifying characteristics of your tail (dress, gait, height, and weight).

2 Keep an eye on your pursuer, but do not look back at him/her.

Use reflective surfaces such as shop windows to see behind you. If you have a makeup case with a mirror, use that.

3 Stay in crowds.

Do not head for home, to a deserted place, or down alleys.

4 Once you are certain that you are being followed, use these methods to shake your tail:

- Enter the front of a store, shop, or restaurant and go out through the back entrance—most restaurants have exits in the kitchen.
- Buy a ticket for a movie, enter after it has started, and leave through an emergency exit before your pursuer enters the theater.
- Use mass transit, and exit or enter the train or bus just before the doors close.

5 If you have not shaken your tail, walk to a police station or call the police from a public place.

Never head for home unless you are certain you are no longer being followed.

Be Aware

- If you are certain your tail is not dangerous, you may want to confront your pursuer in a public place with many people around. Say that you know you are being followed and ask your pursuer why. Use this method only if you feel the person is not dangerous.

CHAPTER 3

GETTING AROUND

HOW TO JUMP FROM ROOFTOP TO ROOFTOP

1   Look for any obstructions if you have time.
You may have to clear short walls, gutters, or other obstacles as well as the space between buildings.

2   Check your target building.
Make certain that you have enough space to land and roll. If the target building is lower than your building, assess how much lower it is. You risk broken ankles or legs if there is more than a one-story differential in the buildings. If there are two stories or more, you risk a broken back.

3   Check the distance between the buildings.
Most people cannot jump farther than 10 feet, even at a full run. If the buildings are farther apart than this distance, you risk catastrophic injury or death. You must clear the distance and land on the other roof, or be able to grab on to a ledge on the other side. If the target building is lower, your forward momentum will continue to carry you even as you fall, so you may be able to leap a greater distance—though probably not more than about 12 feet. You could successfully leap a span across an alley, but not a two-lane road.

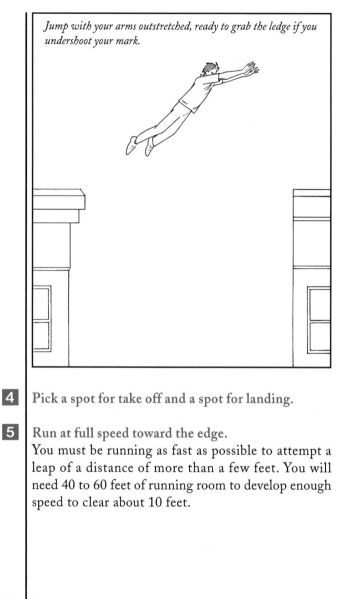

Jump with your arms outstretched, ready to grab the ledge if you undershoot your mark.

4 Pick a spot for take off and a spot for landing.

5 Run at full speed toward the edge.
You must be running as fast as possible to attempt a leap of a distance of more than a few feet. You will need 40 to 60 feet of running room to develop enough speed to clear about 10 feet.

6 Leap.

Make sure your center of gravity is over the edge of your target building in case your whole body doesn't clear the span and you have to grab hold. Jump with your arms and hands extended and ready to grab the ledge.

7 Try to land on your feet, then immediately tuck your head and tumble sideways onto your shoulders, not forward onto your head.

Because you will not be moving fast, it is safe to roll head over heels, unlike jumping from a moving vehicle.

HOW TO JUMP FROM A MOVING TRAIN

1 Move to the end of the last car.
If this is not an option, you can jump from the space between cars, or from the door if you can get it open.

2 If you have time, wait for the train to slow as it rounds a bend in the tracks.
If you jump and land correctly, you will probably survive even at high speeds (70 mph or more), but you increase your chances of survival if the train is moving slowly.

3 Stuff blankets, clothing, or seat cushions underneath your clothes.
Wear a thick or rugged jacket if possible. Use a belt to secure some padding around your head, but make certain you can see clearly. Pad your knees, elbows, and hips.

4 Pick your landing spot before you jump.
The ideal spot will be relatively soft and free of obstructions. Avoid trees, bushes, and, of course, rocks.

5 Get as low to the floor as possible, bending your knees so you can leap away from the train car.

Pick your landing spot, and jump as far away from the train as you can. Protect your head.

Try to land so that all parts of your body hit the ground at the same time.

Roll like a log, keeping your head protected.

6 Jump perpendicular to the train, leaping as far away from the train as you can.

Even if you jump from the last car, leap at right angles to the direction of the train. This way, your momentum will not carry you toward the wheels and tracks.

7 Cover and protect your head with your hands and arms, and roll like a log when you land.

Do not try to land on your feet. Keep your body straight and try to land so that all parts of your body hit the ground at the same time—you will absorb the impact over a wider area. If you land on your feet, you will most likely break your ankles or legs. Do NOT roll head over heels as if doing a forward somersault.

HOW TO ESCAPE FROM A CAR HANGING OVER THE EDGE OF A CLIFF

1 Do not shift your weight or make any sudden movements.

2 Determine how much time you have.

If the car is like the majority of cars, it is front-wheel drive with the engine in front. This means the bulk of its weight is over the front axle. If the rear, rather than the front, is hanging over the edge of the cliff, you probably have more time to climb out. If the front of the car is over the edge, assess your situation. What is the angle of the car? Is it teetering? Does it sway when you shift your weight? If the car is shifting, you must act quickly.

3 If the front doors are still over land, use these doors to make your escape, regardless of which way your car is facing.

Open the door gradually, move slowly, and get out.

4 If the front doors are over the edge, move to the rear of the car.

Proceed slowly and deliberately; do not jump or lurch. If you have a steering wheel lock or a screwdriver, take it with you—you may need it to get out.

If the front doors are over the edge of the cliff, move slowly to the rear of the car and get out.

how to escape from a car hanging over the edge of a cliff

5 Reassess your situation.

Will opening the rear doors cause the car to slide? If not, open them slowly and get out quickly.

6 If you think that opening the rear doors will cause the car to slide over the edge, you must break the window.

Without shifting your weight or rocking the car, use the steering wheel lock or screwdriver to shatter the rear door window (this is safer than breaking the back window because it will require less movement as you climb out). Punch it in the center—the window is made of safety glass and will not injure you.

7 Get out as quickly as possible.

Be Aware

- In situations involving several people, everyone in the front (or everyone in the back) should execute each step simultaneously.
- If driver and passengers are in both front and rear seats, the people who are closest to the edge of the cliff should attempt to get out of the car first.

HOW TO ESCAPE WHEN TIED UP

Upper Torso Bonds

1 When your captors start binding you, expand your body as much as possible.
   - Take a deep breath, puff out your chest, and pull your shoulders back.
   - Flex your arms against the bonds.
   - Push against the bonds as much as possible.

2 When your captors are away, suck in your chest and stomach.

3 Wiggle free with the extra room you have given yourself.

Hand and Wrist Bonds

1 Push or flex against the bonds as your captors are tying you.

2 Keep your wrists apart, if possible.

3 Use a pointed object that protrudes (a spike or hook) to work the bonds loose.
   You may also be able to work the knots free with your teeth by biting and pulling on the knots.

Take a deep breath.

Flex against your bonds.

Keep your wrists apart.

Brace toes and knees together.

4 Free yourself by relaxing your hands and wrists and working until the slack can ride over your palms and fingertips.

Leg and Ankle Bonds

1 While being bound, flex your thighs, knees, calves, and ankles against the bonds.
- If being bound at the ankles, force them apart by bracing the toes of your shoes and knees together.
- If being bound at the thighs or calves, force them apart by keeping the toes of your feet together and your legs turned slightly outward.

2 Relax your legs and work the bonds down.
Use your hands to pull the bonds off your legs and ankles, even if your hands are bound.

Removing Gags

★ Rub your face or head against a wall, a piece of furniture, or anything projecting to slip the gag down over your chin.

HOW TO RAM
A BARRICADE

1 Identify the barricade's weakest point.
The side of the barricade or gate that opens, or the place where a lock holds it closed, is usually its most vulnerable spot. Some barricades and gates have no locks at all: These are opened and closed by the force of an electric motor or magnet, which can be over-powered rather then rammed (see below).

2 Aim for the weak spot.
If possible, use the rear of the car to ram the weak spot—hitting with the front may damage the engine and cause the car to stall.

3 Accelerate to a speed of 30 to 45 mph.
Too rapid an approach will cause unnecessary damage to the car. Keep your foot on the gas all the way through. Consider how much room you will need to turn or stop once you clear the barricade.

4 Duck just before impact if you are heading toward an extremely tall barricade or fence.
Pieces of the barricade may come through your window or the windshield may shatter.

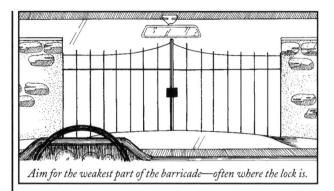

Aim for the weakest part of the barricade—often where the lock is.

5 Avoid poles or anchors that are sunk into the ground.

These may bend and not break, and then drag against and damage the underside of the car, preventing you from driving.

6 Repeat as necessary to break through.

ELECTRONIC GATES

Electrically powered gates that swing open and closed (like those found in gated communities and apartment complexes) are best pushed open rather than rammed. Pushing or forcing the gate open with your car will result in minimal damage and will almost always open the gate. If you are traveling in the direction the gate opens, simply ease your bumper up to the gate and push. Your car will easily overpower the small electric motor that operates the gate.

HOW TO ESCAPE FROM THE TRUNK OF A CAR

1 If you are in a trunk that has no wall separating the backseats and the trunk, try to get the seats down.
Although the release for most seats is inside the passenger compartment, you may be able to fold or force them down from the trunk side. (If not, continue to step 2.)

2 Check for a trunk cable underneath the carpet or upholstery.
Many new cars have a trunk release lever on the floor below the driver's seat. These cars should have a cable that runs from the release lever to the trunk. Look for the cable beneath carpeting or upholstery, or behind a panel of sheet metal. If you locate the cable, pull on it to release the trunk latch. (If not, continue to step 3.)

3 Look for a tool in the trunk.
Many cars have emergency kits inside the trunk, underneath or with the spare tire. These kits may contain a screwdriver, flashlight, or pry bar. Use a screwdriver or pry bar to pry the latch open. You can also pry the corner of the trunk lid up and wave and yell to signal passersby. (If there is no tool, continue to step 4.)

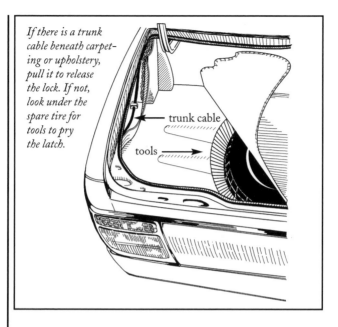

If there is a trunk cable beneath carpeting or upholstery, pull it to release the lock. If not, look under the spare tire for tools to pry the latch.

trunk cable

tools

4 Dismantle the car's brake lights by yanking wires and pushing or kicking the lights out.

Then wave and yell to signal passersby or other cars. This method is also recommended if the car is moving and you need to signal cars behind you.

Be Aware

• No car trunk is airtight, so the danger of suffocation in a car trunk is low. Breathe regularly and do not panic—panic increases the danger of your hyperventilating and passing out. Keep in mind, however, that on a hot day the interior temperature of a car trunk can reach 140 degrees. Work quickly but calmly.

HOW TO SURVIVE
A FALL ONTO
SUBWAY TRACKS

1 Do not attempt to climb back onto the platform
unless you are certain that you have enough time
to do so.
If a train is approaching, you will need to act quickly.

2 Avoid areas of the ground near the track and the wall
that are marked with a strip of tape or with red and
white painted stripes.
Such markings indicate that the train passes extremely
close to these areas, and you will not have enough clearance. In areas with these markings, there should be
alcoves every several yards. These alcoves are safe to
stand in if you can fit within them.

3 If the tracks are near a wall, check to see if there
is enough space to stand between the train and
the wall.
Clearance of $1\frac{1}{2}$ to 2 feet should be enough. Remove
any articles of clothing or bags that could catch on the
train. Stand straight, still, and tall facing the train,
which will pass just inches in front of you.

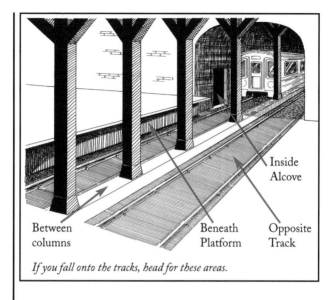

Between columns

Beneath Platform

Opposite Track

Inside Alcove

If you fall onto the tracks, head for these areas.

4 If the tracks are located between the platform and another set of tracks, you may be able to move to the other track instead.

Be mindful of trains approaching on the other side. Cross the third rail (which carries the electric current) by stepping completely over it—do not step on the wooden guard, since it may not hold you.

5 If a line of columns separates the tracks from other tracks, stand between the columns.

Remove any articles of clothing or bags that could catch on the train, and stand straight, still, and tall.

6 Check to see if there is enough space for you to crawl under the lip of the concrete platform and avoid the train.

Use this only as a last resort—this strategy is not recommended since all platforms are different.

Alternatives

If none of these options is feasible, you have two other choices.

- Run past the leading end of the platform, beyond where the front car will stop.

    Since trains running on the track closest to the platform are likely to stop at a station (as opposed to express trains, which usually run on center tracks), you can clear the train by running well past the leading end of the platform and thus the front car. (Note: This method will not work for express trains that only stop at some stations, so you are taking your chances.)

- If there is a depression in the concrete between the rails, lie down into it—there will be enough room for a train to pass over you. (Use this method only in desperation—the train may be dragging something, or there may not be enough clearance.)

HOW TO SURVIVE IN A PLUMMETING ELEVATOR

1 Flatten your body against the car floor.

While there is disagreement among the experts, most recommend this method. This should distribute the force of impact, rather than concentrate it on one area of your body. (Standing may be difficult anyway.) Lie in the center of the car.

Lie flat on the floor in the center of the elevator, covering your head for protection.

2 Cover your face and head to protect them from ceiling parts that may break loose.

Be Aware

- Hydraulic elevators are more likely than cable elevators to fall. These elevators are pushed from the bottom by a giant piston, similar to car jacks at service stations. Because the jack is subject to ground corrosion, it can rot, which could eventually cause the car to fall. The height of hydraulic elevators is limited to about 70 feet, so a free fall would probably result in injury—but not death.

- Elevators have numerous safety features. There have been very few recorded incidents involving death from plummeting elevators. In general, it is highly unlikely for a cable (also called traction) elevator to fall all the way to the bottom of the shaft. Moreover, the compressed air column in the elevator hoistway and the car buffers at the bottom of the hoistway may keep the forces of the impact survivable.

- Jumping just before the elevator hits the bottom is not a viable alternative. The chances that you will time your jump exactly right are infinitesimally small. Besides, the elevator will not remain completely intact when it hits—it will likely collapse around you and crush you if you are in the middle of your jump, or even if you are still standing.

CHAPTER 4

OUT AND ABOUT

HOW TO SURVIVE WHEN LOST IN THE JUNGLE

How to Find Civilization

1 Find a river.
Generally, animal trails will lead you to water. Water is the key to jungle navigation and usually the quickest way to travel.

2 Fashion a makeshift raft using the method on page 93.

3 Let the current carry you downstream.

4 Travel on the rivers only during the daylight hours.
Alligators and crocodiles are generally night hunters, so avoid traveling on water at night.

5 Watch closely for signs of villages or settlements.
Many jungle settlements and villages are located along the shores of rivers.

How to Find Food and Water

★ If you do not have the means to purify water (see page 129 for details), cut sections from large water vines, or cut banana trees (see page 127 for details) and capture the water welling out of the stalks.

To make a raft:

You will need two tarps or ponchos, green brush, two large saplings, and ropes or vines.

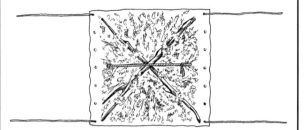

Tie rope to the corners of one tarp. Pile fresh green brush 18 inches high all around. Place two saplings across the brush in an X.

Pile another 18 inches of brush atop the X. Compress the brush. Pull the sides of the tarp tightly around the pile, and tie diagonally.

Place another tarp on the ground. Put the bundle open-side down in the center of the tarp on the ground. Tie tightly as shown. Use the raft rope-side up.

Only drink water from streams and rivers as a last resort, when dehydration and death are a near certainty. Diarrhea will most likely result, so increase your water intake and keep moving.

⭐ If you cannot peel it or cook it, do not eat it.
Avoid brightly colored plants or plants with a milky sap (many of these are poisonous).

Insects, grubs, and raw fish (except those with bristles or spines rather than scales) are safe to eat. Look for grubs and insects beneath rotting logs and vegetation. Pinch the heads off and eat them raw. Peel fruits carefully before eating; the peels may harbor diarrhea-causing bacteria.

How to Travel over Land

- Mark your trail by breaking and turning over fresh vegetation. This will reveal the bright undersides of leaves and will leave a clear trail should you need to backtrack.
- Look for shelter during bad weather. Large hollow tree buttresses can often be used. Line the ground with palm fronds, and stand several more palm fronds over the opening. Note: Do not build this shelter under a tall tree during a thunderstorm because of lightning danger.
- Be prepared for the dangers of the jungle. Most jungle creatures (such as big cats and snakes) want to avoid you as much as you do them. The real danger comes from the smallest creatures: scorpi-

ons, ants, flies, mosquitoes, and the bacteria in water and on fruit. The best defense against bites and stings is to watch where you put your hands and feet. Ants rule the jungle, so do not camp for the night in their line of travel or near nests. Never touch any brightly colored amphibians. Many, like the poison dart frog, have a powerful toxin in their skin, and any contact can make you very ill.

Be Aware

- Before traveling to a remote area, take the time to look at any available maps. Pay attention to topography and any roads or waterways nearby. If you get lost, you will need to know what general direction of travel will intersect a road or waterway and thus, eventually, civilization.

- The jungle canopy can totally occlude the sun, so a compass may be your only means of determining direction. The same heavy canopy will make it impossible for would-be rescuers to find you, or even to locate a downed aircraft. Unlike being lost in a wilderness situation, staying put in the jungle means virtually certain death.

- To make a natural insect repellent, you can use a termite nest. These nests are abundant on the ground and in trees. They resemble irregular-shaped dirt mounds the size of 55-gallon barrels. Break up the mounds (they look like dirt but are actually digested wood) and rub the material on your skin.

HOW TO FIND YOUR WAY WITHOUT A COMPASS

STICK AND SHADOW METHOD

Be aware that the closer you are to the equator, the less accurate this method is.

What You Need:
- An analog watch
- A six-inch stick

Northern Hemisphere

1 Place a small stick vertically in the ground so that it casts a shadow.

In the Northern Hemisphere, place your watch on the ground so that the hour hand is parallel to the shadow. In the Southern Hemisphere, place your watch so that 12:00 is parallel to the shadow.

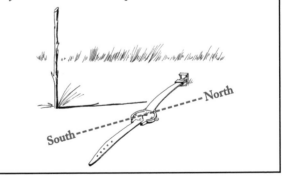

2 Place your watch on the ground so that the hour hand is parallel to the shadow of the stick.

3 Find the point on the watch midway between the hour hand and 12:00.

If the watch is on Daylight Savings Time—which is during most of the summer—use the midway point between the hour hand and 1:00.

4 Draw an imaginary line from that point through the center of the watch.

This imaginary line is a north-south line. The sun will be located toward the south.

⭐ **Southern Hemisphere**

Place your watch on the ground so that 12:00 is parallel to the shadow.

Then find the midway point between the hour hand and 12:00. Draw an imaginary line from the point through the center of the watch. This is the north-south line. The sun will be located toward the north.

Star Method

Northern Hemisphere

⭐ Locate the North Star, Polaris.

The North Star is the last star in the handle of the Little Dipper. Walking toward it means you are walking north. You can use the Big Dipper to find the North Star. A straight imaginary line drawn between the two stars at the end of the Big Dipper's bowl will point to the North Star. The distance to the North Star is about five times the distance between the two "pointer" stars.

Southern Hemisphere

 Find the Southern Cross.

The Southern Cross is a group of four bright stars in the shape of a cross and tilted to one side. Imagine the long axis extends in a line five times its actual length. The point where this line ends is south. If you can view the horizon, draw an imaginary line straight down to the ground to create a southern landmark.

Cloud Method

Look at the clouds to determine which direction they are moving.

Generally, weather moves west to east. While this may not always be true in mountain regions, it is a good rule of thumb and may help orient you.

Moss Method

Locate moss.

Mosses grow in places with lots of shade and water: areas that are cool and moist. On tree trunks, the north sides tend to be more shady and moist than the south sides, and therefore, moss usually grows on the north sides of trees. However, this method is not infallible—in many forests, both sides of a tree can be shady and moist.

HOW TO CLIMB OUT OF A WELL

WITH A NARROW OPENING

Use the "chimney climbing" technique if the opening is narrow enough to keep your back against one wall and your feet against the opposite side, holding yourself off the ground.

1 Place your back against one wall and your hands and feet against the other wall.
Your body will be in an "L" shape, with your back straight and your legs sticking out—the soles of your feet pressing against the opposite wall. If the well is not completely vertical but is tilted in one direction, place your back on the lower wall.

2 Use even, steady pressure from your thighs to maintain traction on the feet and friction on your back, and to hold yourself off the ground.

3 Place the palms of your hands against the wall behind you, below your buttocks.

4 Take your right foot off the opposite wall and place it under your backside.
Bend your leg under you so that your left foot is on one wall and your right is on the other.

To climb out of a well
with a narrow opening:

*Place your back against one
wall and your hands and feet
against the other.*

*Using even pressure to
maintain traction, place your
hands below your rear.*

Take one foot off the wall and place it under your rear.

Push up with your hands.
Repeat step 1 through 4.

5 │ While pressing your back away from the wall with your hands, push up with your hands and your feet. Move only about 6 to 10 inches.

6 │ Place your back on the wall again and move your right foot back onto the opposite wall, now a bit higher than your left foot.
Rest.

7 │ Repeat the procedure, beginning with your left foot. Alternate feet, slowly working your way to the lip of the well.

8 │ When you approach the lip of the well, reach up with your hand overhead and perform a "mantle move."
Pull yourself halfway up from a chin-up hang position, then roll (shift) your weight onto your forearms as they clear the lip of the well. Shift your body weight to your hands, and press up. Use your feet against the wall to assist in pulling yourself up out of the well.

WITH A WIDE OPENING

Use the "spread eagle" or "stemming" technique for an opening that is too wide to use the chimney climbing technique but narrow enough that you can touch opposite walls with your hands.

1 Place your right hand and right foot on one wall and your left hand and left foot on the opposite wall.
Your hands should be lower than your shoulders, and your fingers should point down.

2 Keep the pressure on your feet by assuming a somewhat scissored leg stance, with your body facing slightly to your right.

3 Brace yourself by pushing out with your hands.

4 Move one foot quickly up a few inches, followed quickly by the other.

5 Continue until you reach the top, where you will have to grab something sturdy and swing up over the edge.
If nothing is available to grab onto, keep going until your upper body is out of the well, then flop over forward and use leverage to climb out.

HOW TO NAVIGATE A MINEFIELD

1. Keep your eyes on your feet.

2. Freeze—do not move any farther.

3. Look for spikes, detonators, wires, bumps, or discoloration in the ground around you.

4. Avoid spikes, detonators, wires, bumps, or discoloration in the ground, and back up slowly in your own footsteps.
   Do not turn around. Walk backward.

5. Stop when you are certain you are safe.

HOW TO IDENTIFY AND AVOID MINEFIELDS

The simplest way of avoiding mines is to avoid regions where you suspect they may be, such as post-war countries. If you are in such a region, follow these tips.

- Ask locals.
  Explosive Ordnance Disposal (EOD) technicians, local women, and children are the best sources of information (in that order) for where danger zones are located.

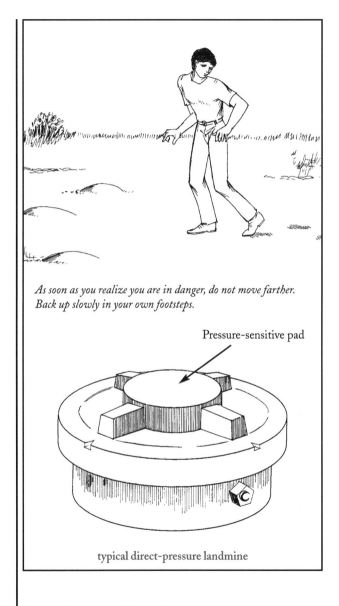

As soon as you realize you are in danger, do not move farther. Back up slowly in your own footsteps.

Pressure-sensitive pad

typical direct-pressure landmine

- Observe animals.
  Field animals are considered de facto mine-sweepers. Fields with large quantities of mutilated animals, untouched by people, may indicate a minefield.
- Watch the movements of locals.
  Locals who avoid perfectly good trails are probably avoiding a mined area. Observe which routes they will not travel on and avoid them. Never travel alone in a suspected mined area.
- Look for dirt that has been disturbed.
  Transference of dirt or discoloration of fields may indicate hasty placement of mines.
- Look for wires across trails.
  Trip wires strung across trails indicate mines or other explosives.
- Look for newly destroyed vehicles on or just off the road.
  Evidence of recent mine detonations includes burning or smoking vehicles and craters. Never assume that because a mine has already detonated the path is clear.
- Avoid brush and overgrown fields and trails.
  These will not be clearly marked with mine clearance signs, and are more difficult to navigate on your own.

Be Aware
- Many mines stay active indefinitely. Be sure to ask for guidance in an area known for mines.

• There are four basic mine types:

TRIP-WIRE MINES. Stepping across a wire attached to the detonator will cause the mine to explode.

DIRECT-PRESSURE MINES. Stepping down on a pressure-sensitive pad will activate the detonator.

TIMER MINES. A timer can be an electrical clock, an electronic digital clock, a dripping/mixing chemical, or a simple mechanical timer that will detonate the mine.

REMOTE MINES. A remote mine can be detonated via an electrical charge across a wire (a "clacker"), via a radio signal, or from a heat or sound sensor.

HOW TO SURVIVE
A RIPTIDE

Riptides, or rip currents, are long, narrow bands of water that quickly pull any objects in them away from shore and out to sea. They are dangerous but are relatively easy to escape.

1 Do not struggle against the current.
Most riptide deaths are caused by drowning, not the tides themselves. People often exhaust themselves struggling against the current, and cannot make it back to shore.

2 Do not swim in toward shore.
You will be fighting the current, and you will lose.

3 Swim parallel to shore, across the current.
Generally, a riptide is less than 100 feet wide, so swimming beyond it should not be too difficult.

4 If you cannot swim out of the riptide, float on your back and allow the riptide to take you away from shore until you are beyond the pull of the riptide. Rip currents generally subside 50 to 100 yards from shore.

5 Once the riptide subsides, swim sideways and back to shore.

To escape a rip current, swim parallel to shore until you are beyond the pull of the rip current.

(Direction of rip current)

Be Aware

- Riptides occur more frequently in strong winds.
- Streaks of muddy or sandy water and floating debris moving out to sea through the surf zone are signs that riptides are present, as are areas of reduced wave heights in the surf zone and depressions in the beach running perpendicular to shore.

HOW TO SURVIVE WHEN YOU FALL THROUGH ICE

1 Breathe steadily.

The shock of hitting the cold water will be great, but remain calm.

2 Turn in the direction from which you came.

You most likely came from the area with the strongest ice.

3 Use your elbows to lift yourself up onto the edge of the hole.

Do not get out yet. Hold yourself in that position. Let as much water as possible drain from your clothing.

Reach out onto solid ice, digging keys or another item into the ice to help your grip. Kick your feet as you pull yourself out.

4 Reach out onto the solid ice as far as possible.
If you have car keys, a comb or brush, or anything that might help you dig into the surface of the ice, use it to help pull yourself out.

5 Kick your feet as though you were swimming, and pull yourself up as you continue kicking.

6 Once on the ice surface, do not stand up.
Stay flat and roll away from the hole. This distributes your weight more evenly and decreases your chances of breaking through the ice again.

HOW TO SURVIVE
IN FRIGID WATER

1 Do not attempt to swim unless it is for a very short distance.

A strong swimmer has a 50-50 chance of surviving a 50-yard swim in 50-degree Fahrenheit water. Swim only if you can reach land, a boat, or a floating object with a few strokes. (Swimming moves cold water over skin, causing rapid cooling. Cold water saps body heat 25 times faster than air of the same temperature, and water any colder than 70 degrees Fahrenheit can cause hypothermia.)

2 If you are alone and wearing a flotation device, assume the heat escape lessening posture (HELP).

Cross your ankles, draw your knees to your chest, and cross your arms over your chest. Your hands should be kept high on your chest or neck to keep them warm. Do not remove clothing. Clothes will not weigh you down but will hold warm water against your skin like a diver's wetsuit. This position can reduce heat loss by 50 percent.

3 If two or more people are in the water and all are wearing flotation devices, assume the "huddle" position.

Two to four people should "hug," with chest touching chest. Smaller individuals can be sandwiched between larger members. This position allows body heat to be shared. Also, rescuers can spot groups more easily than individuals.

4 Keep movement to a minimum.
Increasing the heart rate speeds body cooling. Try to breathe normally.

5 Once you are rescued, look for signs of hypothermia.
Slurred speech and a lack of shivering are signs of severe body temperature loss. Immediately rewarm your body.

IF YOU ARE NOT WEARING A FLOTATION DEVICE

1 Grab anything that floats.
A piece of driftwood, a floating cooler, and a plastic bag full of air all work well as flotation devices.

2 If nothing buoyant is available, float on your back, tread water very slowly, or assume the HELP position (see step 2 above).

3 If you are unable to float or tread water, button the top button of a coat or shirt and splash air and water under the bottom edge of your clothing to trap air.
Trapping air under clothing may help you stay afloat, but can also be dangerous since it increases movement and hence cooling.

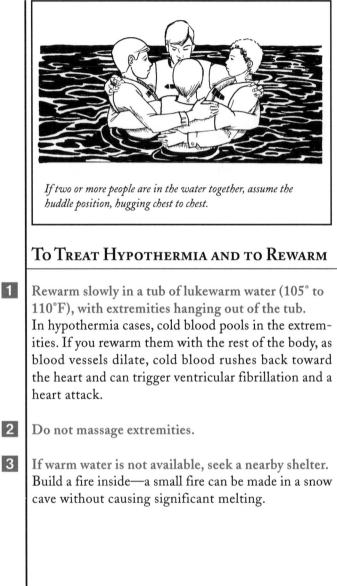

If two or more people are in the water together, assume the huddle position, hugging chest to chest.

TO TREAT HYPOTHERMIA AND TO REWARM

1 Rewarm slowly in a tub of lukewarm water (105° to 110°F), with extremities hanging out of the tub. In hypothermia cases, cold blood pools in the extremities. If you rewarm them with the rest of the body, as blood vessels dilate, cold blood rushes back toward the heart and can trigger ventricular fibrillation and a heart attack.

2 Do not massage extremities.

3 If warm water is not available, seek a nearby shelter. Build a fire inside—a small fire can be made in a snow cave without causing significant melting.

4 Give the victim sugar water, sweets, tea, glucose tablets, or other high-energy, warming foods to restore energy.

Be Aware

- Rewarming through body contact can be dangerous to a single person attempting to warm another—too much body heat may be lost in trying to rewarm the victim, resulting in two people with hypothermia. Use two people if available. Zip two sleeping bags together and put one person on either side of the victim. Keep everyone talking to help spot or prevent loss of consciousness.

HOW TO SURVIVE A TRIP OVER A WATERFALL

1 Take a deep breath just before going over the edge.
You probably will not have much control while you are in the air, and the water may be deep.

2 Go over the falls feet first.
The biggest danger in going over a falls is hitting your head on something underwater and being knocked unconscious. Even feet first there is a risk of broken limbs. Squeeze your feet together and remain vertical.

3 Jump out and away from the edge of the falls just before you go over.
You want to avoid hitting rocks directly at the bottom of the falls.

4 Put your arms around your head to protect it.

5 Start swimming immediately upon hitting the water, even before you surface.
Swimming will slow your descent.

6 Swim downstream, away from the falls.
It is essential that you avoid being trapped behind the waterfall or on the rocks underneath.

Jump away from the edge and go over the falls feet first, covering your head.

how to survive a trip over a waterfall

HOW TO SURVIVE A VOLCANIC ERUPTION

1 Watch out for falling rocks, trees, and debris.
If you are caught amid falling debris, roll into a ball to protect your head. If you are trapped near a stream, watch out for mudflows. (Mudflows are mudslides caused by a large volume of melted snow or ice combined with rocks, dirt, and other debris.) Move up slope, especially if you hear the roar of a mudflow.

If you are caught amid falling debris, roll into a ball to protect your head.

2 If you are in the path of lava, try to get out of its path in any way possible.

You will not be able to outrun the lava, so do not try to race it downhill. If you are near a depression or valley that might divert the flow from you, try to get to the safe side.

3 Move indoors as soon as possible.

If you are already inside, stay there and move to a higher floor, if possible. Close all doors and windows, and move any cars or machinery indoors, if there is time.

4 Do not sit or lie on the floor or ground.

It is possible to be overcome by volcanic fumes. The most dangerous gas is carbon dioxide: It does not have a strong odor, and it is denser than air, so it collects near the ground.

5 Evacuate the area, but only if authorities tell you to do so.

Your best chance of survival is to use a car to drive to a safer area, but even a car may not be fast enough to outpace a lava flow. Some flows travel at 100 to 200 miles per hour. Since volcanic ash can quickly clog the radiator and engine of your car, avoid driving except to evacuate.

Be Aware

Volcanoes can cause all kinds of secondary damage, including mudslides, earthquakes, tidal waves, and dangerous acid rain. If you will be spending time in a volcanic region, have the following emergency supplies at hand:

- Flashlight with extra batteries
- First-aid kit
- Emergency food and water
- Non-electric can opener
- Essential medicines
- Dust masks
- Sturdy shoes
- Goggles
- Portable oxygen tank

FOOD AND SHELTER

HOW TO SURVIVE A HIGH-RISE HOTEL FIRE

Always treat a hotel fire alarm seriously, and exit following hotel procedure. If the fire is nearby, use the following procedure.

1 Feel your hotel room doorknob with the back of your hand.
If the doorknob is hot to the touch, go to step 2 and then skip to step 5. If it is not hot, follow the steps in order.

2 Partially fill the bathtub with cold water.
Soak towels, washcloths, bedsheets, and blankets in the water. If the water is off, use water from the toilet tank. Put a wet washcloth over your mouth and nose and a wet sheet or towel over your head.

3 Open the door.

4 If the hallway is smoke-filled, get as low as possible—one to two feet above the floor.
Make your way to an emergency exit. Never use the elevator.

5 If the door or doorknob is hot, do not open
the door.
Wedge wet towels in the crack under the door to keep
smoke out.

6 Try calling the front desk or rooms on other floors
to check on conditions in other areas.

*If you cannot escape
through the door, make
a tent of wet towels or
sheets at an open window
to protect you from smoke
and to allow you to
breathe outside air.*

7 Turn off fans and air conditioners that could draw smoke into the room, and open the window slightly. If the fire is on a floor below you, smoke may enter the room through the window, so keep the opening narrow. If the fire is not below you, open the window a third or halfway.

8 Make a tent of wet towels and sheets at the window. Do not build the tent if smoke is billowing into the room. Hold or attach one side of the towel or sheet to the window and allow the other side to fall behind you, so you are protected from smoke and are breathing outside air. The towels should help to cool the air and make it easier to breathe.

9 Signal rescue personnel with a white towel or a flashlight.
Wait for rescue.

10 If the air in the room is getting worse, breathing becomes difficult, and no rescue is forthcoming, try to kick through the wall into the adjacent room. Closets are the best locations to try to break through. Sit on the floor of the closet, and knock on the wall until you hear a hollow sound. (Wall studs are normally spaced 16 inches apart.) Use both feet to kick through both surfaces of drywall. You may survive by using this as a breathing hole, or you may need to continue breaching the wall until you can escape into the next room.

11 If you cannot breach the wall, go to a window and look at the outside of the building.

If the rooms have balconies that are close together, consider climbing to another balcony on the same floor. If there are no neighboring balconies, you can tie bedsheets together and climb to a balcony directly beneath yours. Use square knots (the first step in tying your shoes, done twice) and lower yourself one floor only. Consider this option only as a last resort, and only do it if you are attempting to escape an immediate danger or to reach rescue personnel.

Be Aware

- Ladders on fire trucks usually reach only to the seventh floor of a high-rise building. Consider booking a room below this level.
- Poolside or courtyard rooms are likely to be inaccessible to ladder trucks, even if they are below the seventh floor. Consider staying in a streetside room.
- Upon check-in, make sure the hotel has smoke detectors and fire sprinklers.
- Count the doors between your room and the nearest fire exit. This will help you get out safely if smoke reduces visibility.
- Keep your room key where it can be found in the dark.
- Never jump from a height of more than two floors or you risk death.

HOW TO FIND WATER ON A DESERTED ISLAND

1 Collect rainwater in whatever container is handy.
A bowl, plate, or helmet will work—so will a life raft and stretched clothing. In very dry environments, condensation forms on surfaces overnight. Use a tarp or other fabric—shaped as a bowl—to collect water.

2 Collect dew.
Tie rags or tufts of fine grass to your ankles and walk in grass or foliage at sunrise. The dew will gather on the material, which can then be wrung out into a container.

Tie rags to your ankles to collect dew.

3 | Head for the mountains.
An island that appears barren on the coast may have a green, mountainous interior, which is an indication of freshwater streams and creeks. Find these by following trails of vegetation. Do not waste too much energy hiking or moving long distances unless you are relatively certain you will find water (meaning that the lush greenery is not far away).

4 | Catch fish.
The area around a fish's eyes contains drinkable liquid, as do fish spines (except shark spines). Suck the eyes, and break the vertebra of the spine apart and suck the liquid from them. Fish flesh also contains drinkable water—but fish are high in protein, and protein digestion requires additional water, so you are better off squeezing raw fish in clothing or a tarp to extract water.

5 | Look for bird droppings.
In arid climates, bird droppings around a crack in a rock may indicate a water source. (Birds often congregate around cracks where water collects.) Stuff a cloth into the crack, then wring it out into a container or your mouth.

6 | Locate banana and plantain trees.
Cut down the tree, leaving a stump about one foot high. Scoop out the center of the stump, so the hollow is bowl shaped. The roots will continually refill the stump with water for about four days. The first

three fillings will be bitter, but subsequent fillings will be less so. Cover the stump to keep out insects.

Be Aware

- Seawater is generally not safe to drink; its high salt content can cause kidney failure. Moreover, two quarts of body fluid are required to rid the body of the waste in one quart of seawater. As a last resort, you can drink less than 32 ounces of seawater per day; while not healthy, it may keep you alive.
- Rainwater collected in a container is generally safe to drink, provided the container is clean and the water does not stand; any standing water is capable of breeding bacteria.

HOW TO
PURIFY WATER

There are four ways to obtain safe drinking water in the wilderness: filtration, chemical treatment, boiling, and distillation.

FILTRATION

Filter water from all sources in the wild—mountain stream, spring, river, lake, or pond.

1 Find or make your filter.
Coffee filters, paper towels, ordinary typing paper, or even your clothing can serve as filters (the more tightly woven, the better). You can also make an effective filter by filling a sock with alternating layers of crushed charcoal, small crushed rocks, and sand.

2 Pour the water through a filter.
Do this several times to clean out impurities.

Be Aware
• Filtration will only remove some of the water's impurities. It will not kill bacteria or other microorganisms. The best procedure is to filter water first, then treat it with chemicals or boil it.

Chemical Treatment

1 Add two drops of household bleach for each quart of water.
Use three drops if the water is extremely cold or cloudy.

Or

Use one iodine tablet or five drops of drugstore iodine (2 percent) per quart of water.

2 Mix the water and bleach or iodine, and let it sit for at least one hour.
The chemicals will kill microorganisms; the longer the water sits, the purer it will be. Leaving the water overnight is the safest course of action.

Distillation

A solar still uses the heat of the sun to evaporate water trapped in the ground and funnels it into a container for drinking. To build a solar still:

1 Dig a hole about a foot deep, and wide enough to hold your container.

2 Place a clean container at the center of the hole.

3 Cover the hole with a piece of plastic.
A tarp or a section of a garbage bag works well as a cover.

chapter 5: food and shelter

4 Place sticks or stones around the edges of the plastic so that it is flush with the ground and air cannot escape.

5 Poke a $\frac{1}{4}$-inch to $\frac{1}{2}$-inch hole in the center of the tarp and place a small stone next to the hole, so the tarp looks like a funnel.
Make sure the hole is above, but not touching, the top of the container.

6 Wait.
The heat from the sun will cause water in the ground to evaporate, condense on the plastic, and drip into the container. While your solar still will not produce much liquid (less than one cup), the water is safe to drink immediately. The process can take anywhere from several hours to a full day to produce water, depending on the water in the ground and the strength of the sun.

BOILING

⭐ Boil water for at least one minute, plus one minute of boiling time for each 1,000 feet above sea level.
If fuel is abundant, boil water for 10 minutes before drinking it. The longer the water boils, the more microorganisms that are killed. Beyond 10 minutes, however, no further purification occurs. Be sure to let the water cool before drinking it.

HOW TO BUILD A SHELTER IN THE SNOW

BUILDING A SNOW TRENCH

1 Map out a trench so that the opening is at a right angle to the prevailing wind.

You need to find a space large enough so that the width and length are just a bit longer and taller than your body when lying down. You need only a minimal depth to maintain a cozy space for body heat conservation.

2 Dig the trench with a wider, flatter opening on one end for your head, using whatever tools you have or can create.

A cooking pan or long, flat piece of wood works well as an entrenching tool.

3 Cover the top of the trench with layers of branches, then a tarp, plastic sheeting, or whatever is available, then a thin layer of snow.

A "door" can be made using a backpack, blocks of snow, or whatever materials provide some ventilation and yet block the heat-robbing effects of the wind.

BUILDING A SNOW CAVE

1 Find a large snowdrift or snowbank on a slope.
Plan your cave with the opening at a right angle to
the prevailing wind.

2 Dig a narrow tunnel into the slope (toward the back
of the slope) and slightly upward.
Create a cavern big enough to lie in without touching
the sides, roof, or ends.

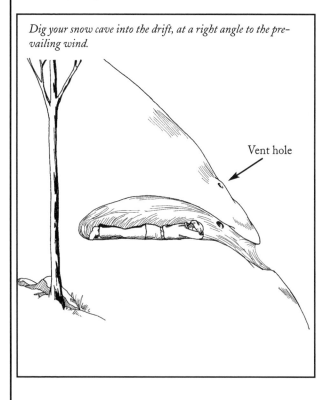

Dig your snow cave into the drift, at a right angle to the pre-vailing wind.

Vent hole

3 Make the ceiling slightly dome-shaped.
A flat ceiling has no strength and will in most cases collapse before you are finished digging. The roof should be at least 12 inches thick. If you can see blue-green light (from filtered sunlight) through the top, the roof is too thin.

4 Put a small vent hole in the roof.
The hole will provide fresh air and a vent for a candle, if you are going to use one. Do not add any heat source larger than a small candle. Excessive heat will cause the ceiling to soften, drip, and weaken.

BUILDING A QUIN-ZHEE

If snow depth is minimal and you have a lot of time and energy, build a Quin-Zhee. A Quin-Zhee is a snow shelter that was developed by the Athabascan Indians, who lived mainly in Canada and Alaska.

1 Pile up a very large mound of packed snow.
The pile needs to be big enough for you to sit or lie down comfortably inside when it is hollowed out.

2 Wait an hour for the snow to consolidate.

3 Dig in and build a snow cave.

Be Aware
• A preferable alternative to building a snow shelter is a man-made structure or vehicle. If none is

available, search for anything that will help protect your body from heat loss. Caves, downed timber, or rock outcroppings can help protect you from the elements.

- If you cannot stay dry in the process of building a snow shelter, or you cannot get dry after you have built it, do not build it! Moving enough snow to create a shelter big enough for even just one person is hard work, and any contact of your skin or clothing with snow while digging will amplify your body's heat losses.

- When building a shelter, the oldest snow will be the easiest to work with, since it consolidates over time.

- Snow is an excellent insulating and sound-absorbing material. From within a snow shelter, you will be unlikely to hear a search party or aircraft. You may want to make a signal above ground that can be noticed by a search party (a tarp, the word "help" or "SOS" spelled out in wood).

- In any shelter, use whatever you can find to keep yourself off the ground or snow. If pine boughs or similar soft, natural materials can be found, layer them a foot or more high, since the weight of your body will compress them considerably.

- When you are inside, the warmth from your body and your exhaled warm air will keep your shelter somewhat comfortable.

HOW TO SURVIVE A TSUNAMI

A tsunami (from the Japanese word meaning "harbor wave") is a series of traveling ocean waves of extremely long length generated by geological disturbances such as earthquakes, underwater volcanic eruptions, and landslides. They can form hundreds or even thousands of miles away. The waves have been known to range from 50 to 100 feet in height. (Tsunamis are often mistakenly referred to as tidal waves, but they are not the same thing. Tsunamis are not related to the gravitational forces which cause tides and, therefore, tidal waves.)

1 If you are near the ocean, be aware of the warning signs of an approaching tsunami:
- Rise or fall in sea level
- Shaking ground
- Loud, sustained roar

2 If you are on a boat in a small harbor and you have sufficient warning of an approaching tsunami, move it quickly.

Your first choice should be to dock and reach high ground. Your second choice is to take your boat far into open water, away from shore where it might be thrown into the dock or the land. Tsunamis cause damage when they move from deeper to more shallow waters; the waves back up against one another at the shallow shelf. Often tsunamis are not even felt in deep water.

3 If you are on land, seek higher ground immediately. Tsunamis can move faster than a person can run. Get away from the coastline as quickly as possible.

4 If you are in a high-rise hotel or apartment building on the coastline and you do not have enough time to get to higher ground away from the shore, move to a high floor of the building.
The upper floors of a high-rise building can provide safe refuge.

Be Aware
- The first tsunami wave may not be the largest in the series of waves.
- Tsunamis can travel up rivers and streams that lead to the ocean.
- Flooding from a tsunami can extend inland 1,000 feet or more, covering large expanses of land with water and debris.

HOW TO SURVIVE A SANDSTORM

1 Wet a bandanna or other cloth and place it over your nose and mouth.

2 Use a small amount of petroleum jelly to coat your nostrils on the inside.
The lubricant will help to minimize the drying of mucous membranes.

Wear a wet cloth or bandanna over your nose and mouth to avoid inhaling sand particles.

3 | All members of a group should stay together.
Link arms or use a rope to avoid becoming separated during the storm and to keep track of group members who might become injured or incapacitated.

4 | If driving in a car, pull off the road as far as possible on the shoulder.
Turn off your lights, set the emergency brake, and make sure your taillights are not illuminated. Vehicles approaching from the rear have been known to inadvertently leave the road and collide with the parked car. Keeping your taillights out will help to avert this danger.

5 | Try to move to higher ground.
Sand grains travel across the surface of the earth mostly by saltation, or bouncing from place to place. Because grains of sand will not bounce high on grass, dirt, or sand, moving to solid high ground is advisable, even if it's just a few feet higher. However, sandstorms can be accompanied by severe thunderstorms, and there may be a risk of lightning. If you hear thunder or see lightning during a sandstorm, do not move to high ground.

Be Aware
- Whenever you are in an area with sandstorm potential (basically, anywhere that there is a lot of sand and wind), wear long pants, socks, and shoes. Because of the way sand moves, your feet and lower legs are more likely to be "burned" by the abrasion of sand than the upper part of your body.

HOW TO CATCH FISH WITHOUT A ROD

1 Determine the best location for your fishing.
Fish usually congregate in shadow, near the edges of lakes, rivers, and streams.

2 Find a forked sapling approximately two feet long. (The forked ends should be approximately one foot long.)
Cut it down or break it off.

3 Bend the two ends toward each other and tie them together.
The tied ends will form the circular frame of a net.

4 Remove your shirt or T-shirt.

5 Tie a knot in the shirt just below the arm and neck holes.

6 Slip the sapling into the shirt, and pin or tie the shirt securely to all sides of the frame.

7 Scoop up the fish.

Alternative
Large fish can also be speared with a pole sharpened to a point at one end. This method works best at night, when fish come to the surface.

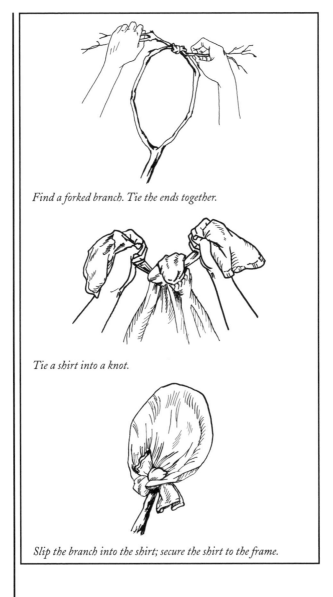

Find a forked branch. Tie the ends together.

Tie a shirt into a knot.

Slip the branch into the shirt; secure the shirt to the frame.

how to catch fish without a rod

HOW TO MAKE ANIMAL TRAPS

Holding Traps

Use a holding trap (or snare) to trap small ground animals. Holding traps capture animals but do not kill them.

1 Procure a two-foot-long wire and a small stick.
Wire is essential—animals can bite through string and twine.

2 Wrap one end of the wire around the stick.
Twist the stick while holding the wire on both sides of the stick with your thumb and forefinger. You will create a small loop around the stick while wrapping the wire around itself.

3 Remove the stick by breaking it near the wire.
Slide the ends out. You will be left with a small loop at one end of the wire.

4 Take the other end of the wire and pass it through the loop.
This will make a snare loop, which becomes a snare that will tighten as the animal struggles. The snare loop should be about five inches in diameter.

5 Twist and tie the end of the wire to a one-foot stake.

6 Place the snare in an animal track or at the entrance to an animal burrow or hole.
You can also use two snares, one behind the other, to increase your odds of catching something. The struggling animal caught in one snare will likely become caught in the other.

7 Anchor the stake in the ground.
Position the stake in an area where the animal won't see it. Mark it so that you can find it later.

8 Check the trap only once or twice daily.
Checking the trap too often may frighten away the animals. When an animal heading for its home becomes caught in the snare, it will struggle to get away, which will tighten the wire trap.

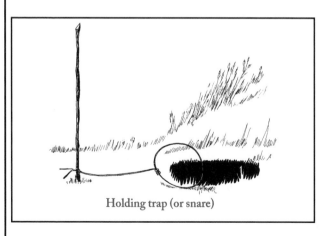

Holding trap (or snare)

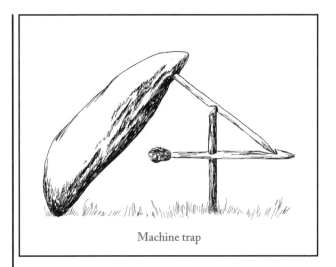

Machine trap

MACHINE TRAPS

Machine traps use gravity, activated by a trigger, to trap or kill animals. The easiest machine trap to build is a deadfall, where a trigger releases a rock or heavy piece of wood to trap or kill an animal.

1 Look for a well-worn animal path on which to place the trap.

2 Find three straight sticks or pieces of wood that are approximately the same length and diameter, and a large, heavy stone or log.
The length and thickness of the sticks you need will depend upon the weight of the stone or log you intend to prop up—use your judgment.

3 | Cut a squared notch in the middle of one stick.
Cut the point of the stick to look like the tip of a flat-head screwdriver—thin and flat. This is your upright support bar.

4 | Cut a squared notch (to fit into the first squared notch like Lincoln Logs) in the middle of another stick.
On this stick, cut a triangular notch a couple of inches from one end, and whittle the other end of the stick to a point. This is your bait bar.

5 | Cut a triangular notch into the middle of the last stick.
This notch should fit on the top of your support stick. Cut one point of this stick to look like the tip of a flat-head screwdriver (to fit into the triangular notch of your bait bar), and cut the other end flat. This is your locking bar.

6 | Anchor your support stick in the ground, perpendicular to the ground.

7 | Attach a piece of meat or food to the end of your bait bar, and insert the bait bar into the notch of your support stick, parallel to the ground.

8 | Place your locking bar on top of your bait and support bar, forming a 45-degree angle with your bait bar.
The screwdriver tip of your locking bar should fit into the notch at the end of your bait bar, and the tip of the support bar should fit into the triangular notch of your locking bar.

9 Lean the stone or log so that the top end rests on the top of your locking bar.

When an animal comes along the trail, it will take the bait, causing the locking bar to dislodge and trigger the deadfall, trapping or crushing your prey.

Be Aware

- To increase the odds of trapping an animal, always set multiple traps, preferably 8 to 10.
- Set the traps where animals live or in areas they frequent, near water and feeding areas. Watch animal patterns to see where they come and go regularly. Dung piles indicate nesting areas.
- Check traps once or twice daily. Dead animals will quickly rot or become food for other animals.
- Do not build the trap where you intend to place it. Build the trap components in camp, then bring them to the place you have chosen. This way, you will not frighten away animals by spending too much time in their habitats. Try to de-scent your traps using leaves or bark to remove your smell.
- Set traps in the narrow parts of animal trails, such as between rocks or in areas with thick brush on either side. Animals will generally only approach traps if there is no easy way around them. Like humans, animals tend to take the path of least resistance.
- Be careful around traps. Animal traps can injure you, and can trap bigger animals than you expect.
- Be alert when approaching any trapped animal. It may not be dead, and it may attack you.
- Do not leave traps or trap elements behind when you leave an area.

CHAPTER 6

SURVIVING ILLNESS AND INJURY

HOW TO DEAL WITH A TARANTULA

Tarantulas are usually not hostile and do not have fatal bites. However, their bites can cause dangerous allergic reactions in some individuals and can be extremely painful, so take care when one crawls on or near you.

1 Find something you can use to brush the tarantula off of you or away from you.

A small stick, rolled newspaper or magazine, or glove works well. Most tarantulas are very skittish, and as soon as you poke them, they will leave in great haste. It is safer to remove the tarantula using an implement than using your bare hand.

2 If the tarantula is on you and cannot be brushed off, stand up carefully and bounce up and down gently.

The tarantula should fall off or skitter away.

How to Treat a Bite

1 Do not panic if you are bitten.

The vast majority of tarantulas give "dry" bites (which look like two pin pricks) first, and then a second bite to inject venom. Avoid *Pterinochilus* and *Heteroscodra*, two species of "baboon spiders" in Africa, and *Poecilothera*, "ornamental tarantulas" in southern Asia, which deliver potent bites.

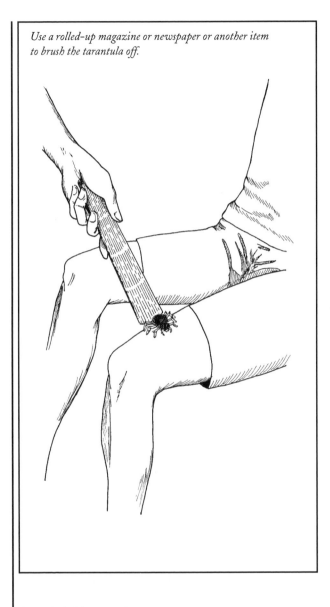

Use a rolled-up magazine or newspaper or another item to brush the tarantula off.

how to deal with a tarantula

2 Treat a dry bite like any other small puncture wound: use an antiseptic to clean it out, and bandage the site quickly.

3 Observe the area around the bite carefully.
A few varieties of tarantula may inject venom that can cause swelling and redness in the area around the bite, as well as pain and tenderness lasting 2 to 6 hours. If these symptoms persist for longer than 12 hours, or if other, more serious symptoms develop, seek medical attention. Unless absolutely necessary, do not drive a vehicle.

4 Treat excessive swelling with antihistamines.
The allergic reaction can be eased with antihistamines, although they are usually slow acting. If symptoms such as extreme flushing in the face, blurred vision, dizziness, profuse swelling around the face or eyes, or restricted breathing occur, epinephrine may be necessary.

5 Watch closely for complications.
While the bite itself is probably not life-threatening, it can become infected, and this is the greatest danger if you are bitten. Seek immediate medical attention if you see signs of tetanus (muscle stiffness, spasm, fever, convulsions, difficulty swallowing, irregular heartbeat, trouble breathing), tularemia (fever, nausea, swollen lymph nodes, sore throat, vomiting, diarrhea), or septicemia (spiking fever and chills, rapid breathing, shock, disorientation, inability to urinate, swollen limbs, blue lips and fingernails).

Be Aware

- Tarantulas are basically just big spiders. Few will bite you unless you try to pick them up.

- Tarantulas are not carriers of any known disease that affects humans or other vertebrates. Tetanus, tularemia, and other diseases that may follow a tarantula bite are most likely the result of post-bite contamination due to unclean environmental conditions. (See step 5.)

- Tarantulas can be found in North America, west of the Mississippi River; in South America; and in warm climates throughout the world. Their habitats vary, and include deep deserts, grassy plains, scrub forests, and rainforests. Most live in burrows, though a few species prefer trees and areas around the base or under the roof of human dwellings.

- Tarantulas are mostly nocturnal and are difficult to notice unless you are searching for them. Most people encounter adult males, which wander during daylight hours looking for female mates.

- Never try to pick up a tarantula. Tarantulas have tough bristles on the tops of their abdomens which can irritate the skin. These come loose easily and float freely through the air. They are shaped like small harpoons with barbed tips and may penetrate the skin and cause a rash or hives.

HOW TO TREAT A SCORPION STING

1 Remain calm.

Scorpion venom induces anxiety in victims, so try especially hard to avoid panic. Most species of scorpion have venom of low to moderate toxicity and do not pose a serious health threat to adult humans, other than severe pain.

2 Apply heat or cold packs to the sting site for pain relief.

The most severe pain usually occurs at the site of the sting. Also use an analgesic (painkiller) if available.

3 If an allergic reaction occurs, take an antihistamine.

Scorpion venom contains histamines, which may cause allergic reactions (asthma, rashes) in sensitive persons.

Scorpion venom induces anxiety in victims.

4 Watch for an irregular heartbeat, tingling in extremities, an inability to move limbs or fingers, or trouble breathing.

Most scorpion stings cause only instantaneous pain at the site of the sting; stings feel similar to those of a wasp. The pain of a scorpion sting may radiate over the body several minutes after the initial sting. Pain tends to be felt in joints, especially in the armpits and groin. Systemic symptoms may also occur—possibly numbness in the face, mouth, or throat; muscle twitches; sweating; nausea; vomiting; fever; and restlessness. These symptoms are normal and not life-threatening, and usually subside in one to three hours. The site of the sting may remain sore and/or sensitive to touch, heat, or cold for one to three days.

5 Seek emergency medical care if you exhibit the above symptoms.

Small children who are stung should seek emergency medical care immediately. Adults, however, have much more time—the odds of dying or even becoming seriously ill as a result of a scorpion sting are extremely slim. You will have at least 12 hours to get to a hospital—probably more.

6 Do not apply tourniquets, as the toxins are small and move extremely rapidly away from the site of the sting.

A tourniquet will not help the wound, and could cause more harm if applied incorrectly.

7 Do not attempt to cut the wound and suck out
the poison.
This can cause infection or transfer the venom into
the bloodstream of the person attempting to remove
the poison.

Be Aware

- Scorpions are active at night, when they hunt
  and search for mates. During the day, scorpions
  hide in burrows or in any available crack or
  crevice, depending upon the species. Scorpions
  are notorious for seeking shelter in objects such as
  shoes, clothing, bedding, and bath towels. Your
  presence may surprise the scorpion and it could
  sting if disturbed. If you are in an area that has
  scorpions, shake out these items before using
  them, and check bedding before sleeping.
- Many species of scorpions will readily enter
  homes and other buildings, which increases the
  likelihood of an encounter. Scorpions will sting
  if surprised or threatened, but generally will not
  sting if unprovoked.
- Scorpions cannot usually deliver enough venom
  to kill a healthy adult. While venom toxicity
  varies among species, some scorpions contain very
  powerful neurotoxins, which, ounce for ounce, are
  more toxic to humans than the venom of cobras.
  However, scorpions inject relatively small amounts
  of venom (compared to snakes), so the overall dose
  of toxins per sting is survivable.

HOW TO CROSS A PIRANHA-INFESTED RIVER

1 Do not cross if you have an open wound.
Piranhas are attracted to blood.

2 Avoid areas with netted fish, docks where fish are cleaned, and areas around bird rookeries.
Piranhas may become habituated to feeding in these areas and may be more aggressive there.

3 Stay out of the water when piranhas are feeding.
When large numbers of piranhas are attacking prey—a true feeding frenzy—they may snap and bite at anything around them. If you see them feeding, stay away, or well upriver.

Piranhas are more active (and hungry) during the day, so cross an infested river at night.

4 Cross the river at night.

Virtually every species of piranha rests at night, and when awakened, will swim away rather than attack. Piranhas are most active at dawn, though some large adults may hunt in the evening.

5 Swim or walk across quickly and quietly.

Try not to create a large disturbance in the water that might awaken piranhas.

Be Aware

- Piranhas are freshwater, tropical fish. In the wild, they exist only in South America, in slow-moving rivers, backwaters, or floodplain lakes. Piranhas generally do not live in either mountain lakes or streams; the water is too cold and flows too fast.
- Piranhas generally do not attack humans or large animals—unless they are already dead or injured. During the dry season, however, when their food supply is scarce, piranhas can be more aggressive. When driving cattle across a river suspected of containing piranhas, farmers will sometimes sacrifice a sick or injured animal downstream before letting the herd enter the water.

HOW TO TREAT A
SEVERED LIMB

1 Locate any individual bleeding arteries on the stump.
The arteries will bleed in pulsating spurts.

2 Pinch off the large arteries that are bleeding the most.
The brachial artery in the arm and femoral artery in the leg carry blood into the limb, and are the major vessels you should find. Someone (the victim or another person) should continue pinching while you proceed to the next step.

3 Apply a tourniquet.
Choose a strip of material at least an inch wide and tie it around the stump as close to the end as possible so that the tourniquet will not fall off when it is tightened. Tie the tourniquet moderately tight but do not immediately cinch it as tight as possible or you may crush and destroy viable tissue. Tighten the tourniquet just enough to stop most of the remaining bleeding. Keep pinching the arteries.

4 Tie off the ends of any blood vessels being pinched.
Use fishing line, dental floss, or heavy thread (in that order of preference) along with a sewing needle if available to carefully tie off the arteries. Pass the line completely around the blood vessel being pinched, as

far up as possible. Tighten the first knot down hard, then place several securing knots on top of the first one. You may want to tie the vessel down in two places, in case one of the stitches comes apart later.

5 Clean the stump thoroughly.
Preventing infection is very important:
- Pick out foreign material lodged in the wound.
- Cut off crushed tissue remnants still attached to the stump. Use a sharp knife or scissors.
- Wash the wound, vigorously irrigating it with a stream of water.

6 Optional: Cauterize remaining bleeding sites.
Using an iron or piece of heated metal, identify the vessels that are still oozing blood. This is simpler during irrigation, when debris and clotted blood are washed away. Dab at each vessel lightly with cloth or gauze to allow yourself to see exactly where its end appears in the wound, then apply cautery at that point. Do not worry about completely eliminating bleeding. If rapid bleeding is well controlled, oozing will be controllable once the dressings are applied.

7 Loosen the tourniquet.
As the pressure from the tourniquet decreases, you will be able to check your ties and ensure more ties (or cautery) are not needed. If bleeding is just a moderate ooze, you have been successful and the tourniquet can be removed. To preserve tissue at the stump, do not leave a tourniquet applied for more than 90 minutes.

8 | Dress the stump.
Coat the end of the stump with any type of available antibiotic ointment (examples include bacitracin, polymyxin, and mupirocin). Then tightly cover the end of the stump with clean cloth or gauze. Elastic strapping works well to hold the dressing onto the stump end. The tighter the dressing, the less the chance of sustained bleeding.

9 | Elevate the stump end as high as possible to allow gravity to assist in slowing further bleeding.

10 | Put an ice pack over the dressing.

11 | Be prepared to apply and tighten a tourniquet again, should heavy bleeding resume.

12 | Treat pain and shock from blood loss.
Use any available pain medication to treat pain from the injury. To treat shock, give the victim animal meat or a liquid containing salt (such as chicken soup). These will help to restore plasma and hemoglobin.

How to Preserve the Severed Limb

1 | Gently wash the severed limb with water.

2 | Wrap the limb in a moist, clean cloth.

how to treat a severed limb

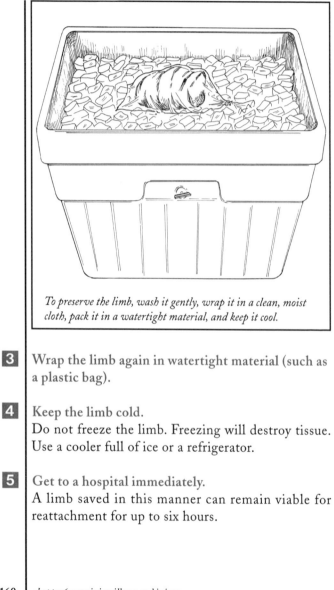

To preserve the limb, wash it gently, wrap it in a clean, moist cloth, pack it in a watertight material, and keep it cool.

3 Wrap the limb again in watertight material (such as a plastic bag).

4 Keep the limb cold.
Do not freeze the limb. Freezing will destroy tissue. Use a cooler full of ice or a refrigerator.

5 Get to a hospital immediately.
A limb saved in this manner can remain viable for reattachment for up to six hours.

Be Aware

- Traumatic amputation of a limb is not necessarily a fatal injury. In order of severity, the immediate problems that you must deal with are rapid severe arterial bleeding; slower bleeding from cut veins; pain; and infection. Only severe bleeding carries an immediate, life-threatening risk, with the possibility of death in minutes.

- Submerging a severed limb in water may cause damage that could hinder its reattachment. You can, however, place it in a watertight container and then submerge that in a river or lake to keep the limb cool.

HOW TO REMOVE A LEECH

1 Do not attempt to remove a leech by pulling up on its middle section or by using salt, heat, or insect repellent.

Dislodging by squeezing, salting, burning, or otherwise annoying the leech while it is feeding will cause it to regurgitate, most likely spreading the bacteria from its digestive system into your open wound, causing infection.

2 Identify the anterior (oral) sucker.

Look for the small end of the leech. A common mistake is to go immediately to the large sucker.

3 Place a fingernail on your skin (not on the leech itself), directly adjacent to the oral sucker.

4 Gently but firmly slide your finger toward where the leech is feeding and push the sucker away sideways.

When the seal made by the oral sucker is broken, the leech will stop feeding. After the oral sucker has been dislodged, the leech's head will seek to reattach, and it may quickly attach to the finger that displaced the head. Even if the oral sucker attaches again, the leech does not begin to feed immediately.

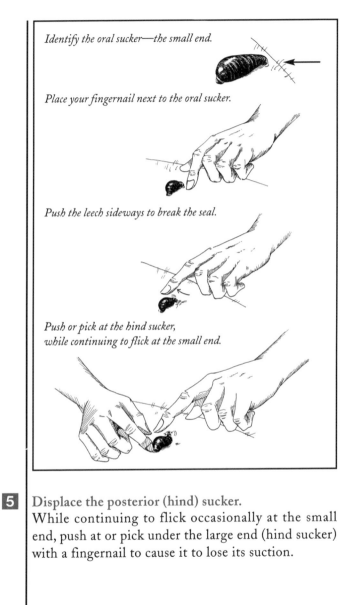

Identify the oral sucker—the small end.

Place your fingernail next to the oral sucker.

Push the leech sideways to break the seal.

*Push or pick at the hind sucker,
while continuing to flick at the small end.*

5 Displace the posterior (hind) sucker.
While continuing to flick occasionally at the small end, push at or pick under the large end (hind sucker) with a fingernail to cause it to lose its suction.

6 Dispose of the leech.
At this point, the leech may have securely attached itself to the finger you used to remove it. Flick it off—it should detach easily. Once the leech is detached, you can put salt or insect repellent directly on it to keep it from attaching to anything else.

7 Treat the wound.
After the leech's anticoagulants lose their effect, the wound should heal quickly. Keep the area clean, and cover it with a small bandage if necessary. Avoid scratching the wound. If itching becomes severe, take an antihistamine.

IF A LEECH INVADES AN AIR PASSAGE

Hirudiniasis is a potentially serious condition in which one or more leeches invade a body orifice. In particular, *Dinobdella ferox* (literally, "the terrifying ferocious leech" or "nasal leech") has a predilection for airways, where it may cause a blockage or asphyxiation, especially if leeches invade the passage in large numbers. If there is a leech invading your airway and you can breathe, do not attempt to remove it—seek medical attention immediately. If you cannot breathe, take the following steps:

1 Gargle with diluted 80-proof alcohol.
Most distilled liquors—vodka, gin, bourbon, scotch—have the requisite alcohol content. Use a mixture of 50 percent alcohol, 50 percent water. Be careful not to aspirate (inhaling the leech and the alcohol).

2 | Spit out the leech.

Alternative

If gargling does not work and the leech is visible, remove it by grasping firmly at the hind sucker and yanking.

Be Aware

- There is virtually no risk of substantial blood loss from leech bites. The wound will continue to bleed for some time after a leech has finished feeding, but this level of blood loss is not dangerous.

- Leeches are generally not known to transmit blood parasites to humans.

- Leeches are more likely to be encountered in still water than in rivers or streams. They are more often found near the edges of clean, clear water than in or near swamps.

- Leeches need a solid surface to hold onto even when they are not feeding. Avoid leeches by staying in the open: Swim in deep, open water, avoid boat docks, and do not wade through areas with submerged branches or rocks. In jungles, remain on trails and be aware of leeches on overhanging branches and vines.

- Both aquatic and terrestrial leeches have incredible senses of perception. They are attracted by vibrations and by body heat, and they have 10 pairs of eyes to detect movement. Keep moving, and check yourself and your traveling companions regularly.

APPENDIX

GENERAL TRAVEL STRATEGIES

⭐ **EMERGENCY INFO**—On a business card, write down emergency contact information and place it in your wallet. Include the names of your doctors, as well as anyone who should be contacted in the event of an emergency. Give your emergency contact a copy of your itinerary, and the name of where you'll be staying.

⭐ **BATHROOM EMERGENCIES**—If you need a bathroom in a hurry, head for the nearest large hotel. Most hotels have bathrooms on or near the lobby that are usually clean and well-kept. Large, expensive hotels are also good for other services—telephones, faxes, e-mail—and will gladly point you in the right direction.

⭐ **FRESHENING UP**—Department stores are great places to freshen up or reapply makeup. Just head for the sample counters and you'll find an array of lipstick, makeup, and perfume at your disposal.

⭐ **TAXIS**—When getting out of a taxi, make sure you leave the door open while you are getting your bags out of the trunk; that way the taxi can't drive off before you get your bags out.

⭐ **HIDING PLACES**—Bras with removable pads are great for hiding money, as are tampon tubes. Not many are willing to invade such private places to find it.

STRATEGIES FOR PACKING

★ **LUGGAGE MARKINGS**—Give each piece of your luggage a unique look—tie a bandanna to a handle or purchase a colored luggage tag. Bags often look alike, and even though you may be able to tell one bag from another, not everyone else is as smart as you are. It will also be easier for you to keep track of your bag from a distance. In lieu of locks, purchase plastic ties to loop through your zippers. These are by no means infallible, but may thwart a thief who is looking for a bag that is easy to open.

★ **CHECKED VS. CARRY-ON**—Pack items you must have with you in transit or upon arrival in your carry-on. Medicine, toiletries, and a change of clothing (or at least underwear) are essentials. Carry with you any items that would be difficult to replace if your luggage is lost or late. Do not risk losing anything valuable in your checked luggage—most airline baggage is insured for only $1,000. If you are traveling with someone you know well, pack half your clothes in their bag and carry half of theirs in your bag. That way, if one bag gets lost, you both have at least half your possessions.

★ **AVOID WRINKLES**—Use plastic dry-cleaning bags between fine garments to keep them from wrinkling. Pack smaller items in zip-lock bags to keep them wrinkle-free.

★ CREATE SPACE—If you run out of space, zip your suitcase and drop it a few times on the floor. This will compress items a bit and free up space.

★ AVOID EQUIPMENT-SPECIFIC BAGS—If you are taking valuable electronic equipment with you (such as cameras, video recorders, or laptops), consider packing them in a diaper or baby bag instead of the fancy, easily identifiable cases designed for them. A diaper bag is less likely to be stolen and has a lot of extra pockets for storage.

★ FALSE WALLET—Prepare a "mugger's wallet" that contains a small amount of money along with a photo ID (not your driver's license or passport) and additional, but replaceable, cards, for bulk. Use this wallet for your daily small expenses, but be prepared to surrender it in an emergency. Carry the wallet in your front pocket, and place a rubber band around it. You will feel any attempt to remove it. Turn it sideways rather than up and down—you will notice more easily if someone tries to remove it.

STRATEGIES
FOR FLYING

⭐ BEST SEATS—For the best seat in the coach cabin, try for a seat in the emergency exit or bulkhead rows. These are assigned on a first-come, first-serve basis at the airport, so get there early. The exit row seats are also obviously some of the safest in the cabin—your nearest exit is no more than a few feet away.

⭐ UPGRADES—Getting upgraded is often as simple as asking at the airport or even on the plane. Although some frequent-flier programs require that you purchase a full-fare ticket in order to use miles for an upgrade, you may be able to obtain a "stand-by upgrade" at the time of your flight if you request it. Just make sure you have your frequent-flier number with you, and that you ask the ticket agent if you can go "stand-by for a first class or business class upgrade." You may be able to get an upgrade by ingratiating yourself with the flight attendants. Some travelers take gifts (cookies, doughnuts) to give the flight attendants upon departure. In other cases, upgrades have been given to passengers who yield their seats to others who might want to sit together. Be nice—not pushy.

⭐ CANCELLATIONS—If your flight is canceled (or if a delay will cause you to miss a later connection and require you to rebook), you are better off calling the airline or your travel agent for immediate rebooking. This way, you won't have to fret in line with the rest of the passengers. As an alternative, go back to the ticket counter at the front of the airport for rebooking if the line at the gate is too long.

Another alternative is to ask that your ticket be endorsed over to another airline that has a more acceptable flight to your destination. Rather than waiting several hours or overnight for the next available flight, seek out a competing airline's schedule, determine if seats are available, and then contact the airline or your travel agent to insist that your ticket be endorsed over to the other airline. Be sure that they route your luggage correctly.

⭐ JET LAG—To beat jet lag, drink a lot of water before, during, and after the flight. Exercise, eat, and sleep well immediately before the trip. Avoid cigarettes and alcohol. Eat lightly in the air. Purchase a small self-inflating pillow to make your sleep more comfortable.

STRATEGIES FOR HOTELS

⭐ **ROOM UPGRADES**—If your reserved room is not available upon arrival, request an upgraded room or another hotel. Also, do not hesitate to complain about broken toilets, dripping showers, or late room service—your stay will be more comfortable when the problem is fixed, and you may get a reduced rate.

⭐ **FINDING YOUR WAY BACK**—If you do not speak the local language, carry a matchbook, card, or brochure with the name and address of your hotel. You can show it to taxi drivers or when asking for directions.

⭐ **SECURITY**—Never use the "Please Make Up My Room" doorhanger in a hotel—it advertises to others that you are not in. Housecleaning will check in and clean your room anyway.

⭐ **DRYING WET CLOTHES**—Hang wet clothes overnight in the bathroom on a coat hanger and leave the light on. They should be dry by morning.

⭐ **CLIMATE CONTROL**—In newer hotels with windows that cannot be opened, the ventilation system may dehydrate you. To avoid waking up with a dry mouth and thirsty feeling, soak a towel in water and drape it over a chair in the room. Place the bottom of the towel in a wastepaper basket. The wet towel will add moisture to the air.

STRATEGIES FOR TRAVEL IN DANGEROUS REGIONS

⭐ **CHECK BEFOREHAND**—The U.S. State Department posts warnings on their website (http://www.travel.state.gov/travel_warnings.html) about recent activities (warfare, terrorism, civil unrest) in all parts of the world.

⭐ **I.D. PICTURES**—If you are traveling with friends, spouses, or children, make sure you all have color pictures of each other in case something happens. Carry a photocopy of your passport identification page and a copy of your credit card numbers in a safe hiding place.

⭐ **DRESS**—Dress conservatively, and do not wear or carry obvious signs of wealth (designer branded clothing, gold watches, expensive jewelry, cameras, CD players, etc.).

⭐ **PHOTOS**—Ask permission before taking pictures; do not try to sneak photos. Do not take photographs of military installations, government buildings, women, the infirm, or the elderly.

FOREIGN EMERGENCY PHRASES

In a foreign land, when a worst-case scenario occurs, it is extremely helpful to know the native language. While we cannot provide you with a complete phrasebook, we have translated several helpful English phrases into **Spanish, French, German,** and **Japanese** (transliterated). Even though the local language may be different from all of these, odds are that you will get your point across if you know these key phrases.

Help!

¡Socorro! (Spanish)

Au secours! (French)

Hilfe! (German)

Tasukete! (Japanese)

Stop, thief!

¡Alto, ladrón!

Arrêtez-vous, voleur!

Halt, Dieb!

Mate, dorobô!

Run!

¡Corre!

Courez!

Lauf!

Nigero!

Is there a doctor/pilot/lawyer in the building?

¿Hay un médico/piloto/abogado en este edificio?

Y a-t-il un médecin/un pilote/un avocat dans le bâtiment?

Gibt es einen Arzt/Pilot/Anwalt im Haus?

Kono biru no naka ni isha/pairotto/bengoshi wa imasuka?

Hello—I have been seriously wounded.

Hola—tengo una lesión grave.

Bonjour—je suis sérieusement blessé(e).

Guten Tag—ich bin schwer verletzt worden.

Konnichiwa—watashi wa ôkega wo shite imasu.

I am bleeding profusely.

Estoy sangrando mucho.

Je saigne abondamment.

Ich blute stark.

*Watashi wa obitadashiku chi ga
dete imasu.*

May I use your belt as a tourniquet?

*¿Podría yo usar su cinturón para un
torniquete?*

*Je peux utiliser votre ceinture comme
tourniquet?*

*Darf ich Ihren Gürtel als Aderpresse
benutzen?*

*Anata no beruto wo karite
shiketsutai ni shitemo iidesuka?*

**May I borrow a towel to wipe up
the blood?**

*¿Me presta una toalla para limpiar
la sangre?*

*Je peux emprunter une serviette pour
éponger le sang?*

*Darf ich ein Tuch borgen,
um das Blut abzuwischen?*

*Taoru wo karite chi wo fuite
mo iidesuka?*

**Would you please take me to a
clean hospital?**

*¿Me podría llevar a un hospital
bueno?*

*Pourriez-vous m'emmener à un
hôpital propre, s'il vous plaît?*

*Würden Sie mich bitte in ein sauberes
Krankenhaus bringen?*

*Kirei na byôin ni tsurete itte
kudasai masuka?*

Is this safe to eat?

¿Se puede comer?

On peut manger ceci sans danger?

*Sind Sie sicher, dass man das
essen kann?*

Kore wo tabetemo daijôbu desuka?

**Why is the water
brown/green/black?**

*¿Por qué es turbia/verde/negra
el agua?*

*Pourquoi l'eau est-elle
brune/verte/noire?*

*Warum ist das Wasser
braun/grün/schwarz?*

*Kono mizu wa dôshite
chairoin desuka/midori iro
nandesuka/kuroin desuka?*

What kind of meat is this?

¿Qué tipo de carne es ésta?

Quel type de viande est-ce que c'est?

Was für Fleisch ist das?

Kore wa nanno niku desuka?

**I am sorry—I did not mean to
offend you.**

*Lo siento—no quise ofenderlo/
ofenderla.*

*Je suis désolé(e)—je ne cherchais pas à
vous offenser.*

*Es tut mir leid—ich wollte Sie nicht
beleidigen.*

*Gomennasai—anata no kibun wo
gaisuru tsumori wa
arimasen deshita.*

Please do not injure me.
Por favor, no me lastime.
Ne me blessez pas, s'il vous plaît.
Verletzen Sie mich bitte nicht.
Watashi wo itai me ni awasenaide kudasai.

Do not make me angry.
No me enoje.
Ne me fachez pas.
Ärgern Sie mich nicht.
Okoraseruna yo.

I do not wish to hurt you.
No le quiero hacer daño.
Je n'ai pas l'intention de vous blesser.
Ich will Ihnen nicht weh tun.
Anata wo itai me ni awasetaku arimasen.

Is it bleeding much?
¿Está sangrando mucho?
Ça saigne beaucoup?
Blutet es stark?
Chi wa takusan dete imasuka?

Please forgive me, and accept this money/camera/watch as a gift.
Disculpe, por favor, y acepte este dinero/esta cámara/este reloj como regalo.
Pardonnez-moi, et veuillez accepter cet argent/cet appareil-photo/cette montre comme cadeau.
Bitte verzeihen Sie mir, und akzeptieren Sie dieses Geld/diese Kamera/diese Uhr als Geschenk.
Kono okane/kamera/tokei wo owabi no shirushi toshite uketotte watashi wo yurushite kudasai.

Where is the nearest embassy/ airport/hospital/police station?
¿Dónde está la embajada/aeropuerto/hospital/estación de policía más cercano a?
Où se trouve l'ambassade/l'aeroport/ l'hôpital/la gendarmerie le/la plus proche?
Wo ist die nächste Botschaft/der nächste Flughafen/das nächste Krankenhaus/das nächste Polizeiamt?
Ichiban chikai taishikan/kûkô/ byôin/kôban wa dokodesuka?

Yes, I have my papers.
Sí, tengo mis documentos.
Oui, j'ai mes papiers.
Ja, ich habe meine Papiere.
Hai, shorui wo motteimasu.

Where are your papers?
¿Dónde están tus documentos?
Où sont vos papiers?
Wo sind Ihre Papiere?
Anata no shorui wa dokodesuka?

I'm not going to tell you.
No se lo voy a decir.
Je ne vous dirai pas.
Ich sage es Ihnen nicht.
Anata niwa oshiemasen.

**Do you know a place where
    I can hide?**
¿Sabe usted dónde puedo esconderme?
*Vous connaissez un endroit où je peux
    me cacher?*
*Wissen Sie, wo ich mich verstecken
    kann?*
*Dokoka watashi ga kakure rareru
    tokoro wo shitte imasuka?*

How fast can this car go?
*¿A cuánta velocidad puede ir
    este coche?*
*À quelle vitesse cette voiture peut-elle
    rouler?*
Wie schnell kann dieses Auto fahren?
*Kono kuruma wa doregurai hayaku
    hashiremasuka?*

How quickly can you leave?
¿Se puede ir lo más pronto posible?
*En combien de temps pouvez-vous
    partir au plus vite?*
*Wie schnell können Sie mich von hier
    wegbringen?*
Doregurai hayaku deraremasuka?

How far is it to the border?
¿A qué distancia está la frontera?
C'est quelle distance à la frontière?
Wie weit ist es bis zur Grenze?
Kokkyô made doregurai desuka?

You will never make me talk.
Usted nunca me hará hablar.
Vous ne me ferez jamais parler.
*Sie werden mich nie zum Sprechen
    bringen.*
*Zettai watashi wo shaberaseru koto
    wa dekinai.*

GESTURES TO AVOID

THE UPSIDE-DOWN GLASS ON BAR

In the United States and other countries, turning your glass upside-down might indicate that you do not want anything to drink. In some pubs in Australia, however, finishing your drink, turning the glass upside-down, and placing it squarely on the bar may signal that you believe you can win a fight with anyone present.

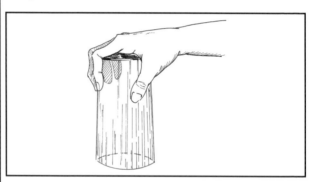

EYE CONTACT

In Pakistan, staring is common. Do not be offended if someone stares at you.

In Zimbabwe, do not maintain continued direct eye contact. It is considered rude, particularly in rural areas.

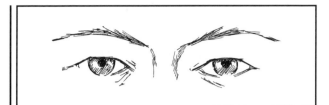

In New York City, do not make eye contact with anyone on a subway, train, or bus. Read a book or newspaper, or maintain an unfocused, nonresponsive visage to avoid incident.

THE FIG GESTURE

The fig gesture is formed by making the hand into a fist and protruding the thumb upward between the forefinger and middle finger. In most Latin American countries it is considered phallic and very rude. In Brazil, the fig gesture means "good luck." In parts of the United States, it means "I've got your nose," part of a children's game in which one person pretends to have captured the other person's nose.

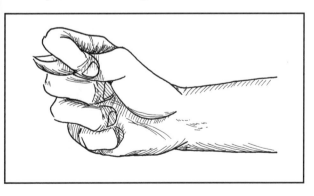

The "OK" Sign

Touching the thumb and index finger to suggest a circle, with the other fingers on the hand fanned out, indicates that everything is okay in the United States.

In Brazil, Germany, and Russia, however, it indicates a very private orifice and is an insult.

In Japan, the sign indicates that you want change. Use this gesture if you want a cashier in a store to give your change in coins.

In France, it is an insult. It denotes the number zero or the concept of something being worthless. When placed over the nose, it means "drunk."

ABOUT THE EXPERTS

FOREWORD
Source: David Concannon, a fellow of The Explorers Club and chairman of its legal Committee, has traveled extensively on four continents, usually with great success. He recently made three deep submersibles dives to the R.M.S. *Titanic*, at a depth of 12,500 feet, including the first dive of the century on July 29, 2000.

CHAPTER I: GETTING THERE

How to Control a Runaway Camel
Source: Philip Gee, safari operator, runs Explore the Outback, a safari group that leads nature tours of Australia on camelback (www.austcamel.com.au/explore.htm).

How to Stop a Runaway Passenger Train
Source: Tom Armstrong has more than 25 years of railway experience. He has been a locomotive engineer since 1977, and served as accident prevention coordinator for the Canadian Pacific Railway. He lives in Saskatoon.

How to Stop a Car with No Brakes
Source: Vinny Minchillo, demolition derby driver, has written for a variety of automobile magazines, including *AutoWeek*, *SportsCar*, and *Turbo*. When not smashing cars, he is the creative director of an advertising agency in Dallas.

How to Stop a Runaway Horse
Sources: John and Kristy Milchick, horse trainers, own and manage Hideaway Stables, a horse farm in Kentucky, where they breed, train, and sell foundation American Quarter Horses. They also publish articles on horse care and training on their website, www.hideawayhorses.com.

How to Crash-Land a Plane on Water
Sources: Arthur Marx, a flight instructor, has been a pilot for 20 years and owns Flywright Aviation, a flight training and corporate flying service on Martha's Vineyard. He is ATP certified and has single- and multi-engine and instrument instruction ratings; Tom Claytor, bush pilot, is currently attempting a solo flight around the world to seven continents (read about it at www.claytor.com). He is a fellow of The Explorers Club, a subject of the National Geographic Special *Flight Over Africa,* and a recipient of the 1993 Rolex Award for Enterprise.

How to Survive an Airplane Crash
Source: William D. Waldock, professor of Aeronautical Science at Embry-Riddle Aeronautical University and associate director of the Center for Aerospace Safety Education at ERAU-Prescott, Arizona, has completed more than 75 field investigations and over 200 accident analyses. He manages the Robertson Aviation Safety Center and has been flying actively in general aviation for more than 20 years.

CHAPTER 2: PEOPLE SKILLS

How to Survive a Riot
Source: The Chief Consultant of Real World Rescue (who must remain anonymous) has more than 20 years of special operations and counter-terrorism experience. Real World Rescue is a small, high-risk travel security company based in San Diego that trains elite U.S. Government Special Operations personnel and Federal law enforcement agents on international terrorism and Third World survival. The company is on the Web at www.realworldrescue.com.

How to Survive a Hostage Situation
Source: The Chief Consultant of Real World Rescue.

How to Pass a Bribe
Source: Jack Viorel, teacher, has lived and worked throughout Central and South America. He currently lives in Northern California.

How to Foil a Scam Artist
Source: Steve Gillick, executive director of the Canadian Institute of Travel Counselors-Ontario, is the author of *Defining Travel Common Sense* and *Son of Scam*, two travel booklets available from www.citcontario.com.

How to Foil a UFO Abduction
Source: The Society for the Preservation of Alien Contact Evidence and Geographic Exploration (SPACEAGE), a grassroots organization dedicated to preserving the nation's extraterrestrial points of interest. The society is the author of *UFO USA: A Traveler's Guide to UFO Sightings, Abduction Sites, Crop Circles, and Other Unexplained Phenomena.*

How to Survive a Mugging
Source: George Arrington, self-defense instructor, has taught classes in self-defense for more than 25 years. He holds a 4th-degree Black Belt and formal teaching license in Danzan-Ryu Jujutsu and has also studied Karate, Aikido, T'ai-chi Ch'uan, Pa Kua, and Hsing-I.

How to Tail a Thief
Sources: Robert Cabral, self-defense instructor, is the founder of The International Academy of Martial Arts in West Los Angeles. He has served as a police defensive tactics trainer and worked for 10 years as a bodyguard in Hollywood. He holds Senior Masters credentials in karate under The Okinawan Karate Federation; Brad Binder,

Ph.D., is vice president of W.R. Associates, Inc., a security firm based in Wisconsin. He has served as a private investigator and protective escort and provides security consultations for individuals and corporations.

How to Lose Someone Who Is Following You
Sources: Robert Cabral; Brad Binder.

CHAPTER 3: GETTING AROUND

How to Jump from Rooftop to Rooftop
Source: Christopher Caso, stuntman, has produced and performed high-fall stunts for numerous movies, including *Batman and Robin*, *The Lost World*, and *The Crow: City of Angels*.

How to Jump from a Moving Train
Source: Christopher Caso.

How to Escape from a Car Hanging over the Edge of a Cliff
Source: Christopher Caso.

How to Escape When Tied Up
Sources: Tom Flanagan ("The Amazing Flanagan"), magician and escape artist; *The Book of Survival* by Anthony Greenburg.

How to Ram a Barricade
Source: Vinny Minchillo.

How to Escape from the Trunk of a Car
Source: Janette E. Fennell, founder of Trunk Releases Urgently Needed Coalition (TRUNC), a nonprofit whose mission is to make sure children and adults trapped in trunks can safely escape. Interior trunk-release regulations based on her work go into effect in 2001.

How to Survive a Fall onto Subway Tracks
Source: Joseph Brennan, author of *The Guide to Abandoned Subway Stations (Disused or Unused Underground Railway Stations of the New York Area)*, at www.columbia.edu/~brennan. He works in the Academic Technologies Group of Academic Information Systems at Columbia University.

How to Survive in a Plummeting Elevator
Sources: Jay Preston, CSP, PE, is a general safety engineering consultant and a forensic safety engineering specialist. He is a former president of the Los Angeles chapter of the American Society of Safety Engineers; Larry Holt is senior consultant at Elcon Elevator Controls and Consulting in Prospect, Connecticut.

CHAPTER 4: OUT AND ABOUT

How to Survive When Lost in the Jungle
Source: Jeff Randall and Mike Perrin, survival experts, run Randall's Adventure and Training (www.jungletraining.com), a service which guides extreme expeditions and facilitates training in the jungles of Central America and the Amazon. They have both completed the Peruvian military's jungle survival school for downed pilots in the Amazon.

How to Find Your Way without a Compass
Sources: Jeff Randall and Mike Perrin; *The U.S. Army Survival Manual*.

How to Climb out of a Well
Source: Andrew P. Jenkins, Ph.D., WEMT, professor of Community Health and Physical Education at Central Washington University, is trained in exercise physiology, wilderness emergency medicine, and mountain rescue; John Wehbring, mountaineering instructor and a member of the San Diego Mountain Rescue Team, is a former chairman of

about the experts

the Mountain Rescue Association (California region). He has taught the Sierra Club's Basic Mountaineering course; Jon Lloyd, an adventure consultant with VLM Adventure Consultants in the United Kingdom, provides adventure sport activities for individuals, youth groups, independent and state schools, company groups and special needs groups (www.vlmadventureconsul tants.co.uk).

How to Navigate a Minefield
Source: The Chief Consultant of Real World Rescue.

How to Survive a Riptide
Sources: The National Weather Service in Miami, FL; Dr. Robert Budman, M.D. ("The Surf Doctor"), an American Board of Family Practice certified physician and *Surfer* magazine's medical advisor; the California Surf Life-Saving Association.

How to Survive When You Fall through Ice
Source: Tim Smalley, Boating and Water Safety Education Coordinator for the Minnesota Department of Natural Resources.

How to Survive in Frigid Water
Source: Tim Smalley.

How to Survive a Trip over a Waterfall
Sources: Jon Turk, author of *Cold Oceans: Adventures in Kayak, Rowboat, and Dogsled*, www.coldoceans.com. He has traveled the Northwest Passage by sea kayak and conquered Baffin Island and the Canadian Arctic by dogsled. He made the successful trip around Cape Horn in a sea kayak a day after his 51st birthday; Christopher Macarak, kayak instructor, owns Paddle TraX Kayak Shop in Crested Butte, Colorado.

How to Survive a Volcanic Eruption
Sources: Scott Rowland, Ph.D., volcanologist and the editor and publisher of the *Hawaii Center for Volcanology Newsletter;* the U.S. Geological Society.

CHAPTER 5: FOOD AND SHELTER

How to Survive a High-Rise Hotel Fire
Source: David L. Ziegler, president of Ziegler & Associates, a security consulting firm concentrating on fire and arson investigation (www.ziegler-inv.com). Formerly an agent with the Federal Bureau of Alcohol, Tobacco & Firearms specializing in fire, arson, and explosion cases, he is a certified fire investigator and a member of the International Association of Arson Investigators (IAAI); John Linstrom, executive director of the Fire & Emergency Television Network, which provides training, information, and education for 240,000 emergency personnel via satellite, videotape, and the Internet. He has degrees in Fire Protection Administration and Fire Science, and is certified as a Master Firefighter, Master Inspector, Fire Instructor, Fire Investigator, Fire Officer, and Emergency Medical Technician.

How to Find Water on a Deserted Island
Sources: Jean-Philippe Soule, leader of the Central American Sea Kayak Expedition and former member of the elite French Mountain Commando Unit; Benjamin Pressley, founder of Windsong Primitives, staff editor at *Backwoodsman* magazine, the Southeastern U.S. field editor for *Wilderness Way* magazine, and webmaster of www.perigree.net/~benjamin/index.htm; *The U.S. Army Survival Manual.*

How to Purify Water
Source: Andrew P. Jenkins.

about the experts

How to Build a Shelter in the Snow
Source: John Lindner, director of the Wilderness Survival
School for the Colorado Mountain Club, is also director
of training for the Snow Operations Training Center, an
organization that teaches mountain survival skills to
utility companies, search and rescue teams, and government
agencies.

How to Survive a Tsunami
Source: Eddie Bernard, Ph.D., is director of the Pacific
Marine Environmental Laboratory, leader of the U.S. team
in the 1993 Sea of Japan tsunami damage survey, and direc-
tor of the Pacific Tsunami Warning Center; the National
Tsunami Hazard Mitigation Program; the NOAA Tsunami
Research Program; the International Tsunami Information
Center.

How to Survive a Sandstorm
Source: Thomas E. Gill, adjunct professor in the Depart-
ment of Geosciences, and a research associate at the Wind
Engineering Research Center of Texas Tech University, and
Jeffrey A. Lee, associate professor in the Department of
Economics and Geography at Texas Tech. Gill and Lee are
members of the Texas Wind Erosion Research PersonS
(TWERPS), an informal research group of scientists and
engineers from the U.S. Department of Agriculture and
Texas Tech who study blowing sand and dust storms; the
Office of Meteorology, National Weather Service; the U.S.
Army Medical Research & Material Command.

How to Catch Fish without a Rod
Source: Jean-Philippe Soule.

How to Make Animal Traps
Source: Ron Hood, survival expert, received his early wilderness training while a member of the U.S. Army and taught wilderness survival classes for 20 years. Currently, he and his wife, Karen, produce wilderness survival training videos.

CHAPTER 6: SURVIVING ILLNESS AND INJURY

How to Deal with a Tarantula
Source: Stanley A. Schultz, president of the American Tarantula Society, is the author of the *Tarantula Keeper's Guide, 2nd edition*. He and his wife/co-author Marguerite live in Calgary and currently own approximately 350 tarantulas.

How to Treat a Scorpion Sting
Source: Scott Stockwell, a major in the United States Army, works as a combat medical entomologist, consulting on scorpion envenomation. By his own reckoning, he has probably been stung by more species of scorpion and other venomous arthropods than any other living person. He holds a Ph.D. in entomology from the University of California, Berkeley, and works in Fort Sam Houston, Texas.

How to Cross a Piranha-Infested River
Source: Paul Cripps, director of Amazonas Explorer, an organization specializing in adventure travel in Peru and Bolivia. He has guided trips through the Amazon for 13 years; Dr. David Schleser, researcher and eco-travel guide, has researched piranhas and led eco-tours to the Brazilian and Peruvian Amazon. He is the author of *Piranhas: Everything About Selection, Care, Nutrition, Diseases, Breeding, and Behavior (More Complete Pet Owner's Manuals)*; Barry Tedder, marine biologist and jungle survival expert, raises piranhas and has studied them in the southern Amazon. He serves in the New Zealand Royal Navy;

Dr. Peter Henderson, director of Pisces Conservation Ltd. in Lymington, England, has worked on piranha and other South American fish for more than 20 years (www.irchouse.demon.co.uk).

How to Treat a Severed Limb
Source: Dr. James Li, practitioner in the Division of Emergency Medicine at Harvard Medical School in Cambridge, Massachusetts, is an instructor for the American College of Surgeon's course for physicians, Advanced Trauma Life Support. He is the author of articles on emergency practice in remote settings.

How to Remove a Leech
Source: Mark E. Siddall is assistant curator for the Division of Invertebrate Zoology at the American Museum of Natural History in New York City.

APPENDIX

Foreign Emergency Phrases
Sources: French: Jennifer Wolf, MA, doctoral candidate in Comparative Literature, University of Pennsylvania; German: Lisa Marie Anderson, MA, doctoral candidate in Germanic Languages and Literatures, University of Pennsylvania; Japanese: William M. Hammell, MA, Japanese Literature, Yale University; Spanish: Paul Carranza, MA, doctoral candidate in Comparative Literature, University of Pennsylvania.

Gestures to Avoid
Source: Roger E. Axtell, author of *Gestures: Do's and Taboos of Body Language Around the World* and seven other books in his *Do's and Taboos* series. He is also a popular speaker on the after-dinner circuit.

ABOUT THE AUTHORS

Joshua Piven, a computer journalist and freelance writer by day, is a continent hopper by night. He has been chased by knife-wielding motorcycle bandits, stuck in subway tunnels, robbed and mugged, and is consistently served pasta when they run out of the chicken. He is the co-author of *The Worst-Case Scenario Survival Handbook*, and lives in Philadelphia with his wife.

David Borgenicht, a writer, editor, businessman and world traveler, has canoed in alligator breeding ponds, ridden elephants in India, stowed away on Amtrak, and almost always gets the exit row in which the seats don't recline. He is the co-author of *The Worst-Case Scenario Survival Handbook*, and author of *The Jewish Mother Goose* (Running Press, 2000) and *The Little Book of Stupid Questions* (Hysteria, 1999). He, too, lives in Philadelphia with his wife, who is still his best-case scenario.

Brenda Brown is a freelance illustrator and cartoonist whose work has appeared in many books and major publications, including *The Worst-Case Scenario Survival Handbook, Reader's Digest, The Saturday Evening Post, The National Enquirer,* and *Federal Lawyer and National Review.* Her digital graphics have been incorporated into software programs developed by Adobe Systems, Deneba Software, Corel Corp, and many websites.

Check out www.worstcasescenarios.com for updates, new scenarios, and more! Because you just never know. . . .